EVALUATING IN-SERVICE TRAINING FOR TEACHERS

2

Evaluating In-service Training for Teachers
Edited by Colin McCabe

This work is based on a text prepared for the
Centre for Educational Research and Innovation
of the Organization for Economic Co-operation
and Development

NFER Publishing Company

Erratum

Evaluating In-Service Training for Teachers

The headings to the two contributions by Euan S. Henderson, beginning on pp.62 and 69 should be transposed.

Note 2 on p.75 refers to the two articles *The Evaluation of an Open University Course* pp.69-75 and *The Evaluation of Short Courses using a Questionnaire*, pp.62-8

© Colin McCabe 1980

Published by the NFER PUBLISHING COMPANY LTD.,
Darville House, 2 Oxford Road East, Windsor SL4 1DF.

Reproduced from copy supplied
printed and bound in Great Britain
by Billing and Sons Limited and Kemp Hall Bindery
Guildford, London, Oxford, Worcester

ISBN 0 85633 205 4

CONTENTS

ACKNOWLEDGEMENTS

I am grateful to the Centre for Educational Research and Innovation of the Organization for Economic Cooperation and Development for stimulating and commissioning the study which is the foundation of this book. Their permission to publish it in this form is appreciated. In particular the lively encouragement and help of M. P. Laderriere must be acknowledged.

I am grateful also to those who have discussed their work with me and to the contributors of the chapters and case studies. Some of the material has already been printed in article or book form so detailed acknowledgements are given in the text.

INTRODUCTION

As part of its work on in-service education and training (INSET) the Organization for Economic Cooperation and Development commissioned a report on the evaluation of INSET in the United Kingdom. The report outlined the provision made in this country and drew together case-studies to illustrate different forms of evaluation which have been carried out. It was presented at a meeting in Paris, held in November 1978, and forms the basis of this volume. Recognition of the need to stimulate, support and provide for teachers' professional development has led to much greater emphasis being placed upon the provision of in-service courses and opportunities for further learning. As the investment grows so does the need to be assured that all the effort and expenditure are worthwhile and for the good of teachers and their pupils.

Evaluation concerns and involves everyone in education. It may be, as Shipman (1979) suggests, a basic management tool in all organizations, but when applied to teachers' professional development through in-service work it becomes more than this, and its procedures and techniques concern and involve everyone in the enterprise. Reports or handbooks on evaluation are needed for teachers, and others working in schools, for whom the in-service provision is intended; for those who train or advise the teachers; for policy decision makers and the managers of that policy.

All of these groups need to be informed: teachers so that they do not feel threatened by evaluation, and so that they can participate fully in its processes and grow professionally, knowing that it gives them a better chance of being responsible for that growth; advisers and trainers so that they can work more closely and cooperatively with teachers; policy decision makers so that they can judge what influence evaluation reports should have; managers so that they can make the best executive and immediate financial decisions about course provision and assessment.

This study is intended, then, to give useful information about what has been done to develop the evaluation of INSET in the United Kingdom. It tries to show something of the theories, principles and assumptions underlying current debates and practices, largely through practical examples of how specific types of investigation can be tackled. Long, short and Open University courses are all referred to. It is not free from the corruption of educational fantasy described by Wilson (1979), but indicates how approaches may be combined and acceptable balances achieved in this important field.

The first part of the book looks at a range of principles and ideas underlying an approach to evaluation in the field, and Taylor surveys some
evaluation studies which have been carried out in the UK. Bolam then reviews relevant literature and experience before highlighting some of the
main issues and implications for national policy. The second part consists
of seven case studies selected to show what sort of evaluation is being
practised in different contexts, and a final discussion.

LIST OF ABBREVIATIONS

ATO   Area training organization: The former co-ordinating bodies for teacher education in an area, often based upon a university institute. They are being replaced by regional bodies.

BEd   Bachelor of Education Degree: In England a degree course which combines the study of probably two other subjects with Educational Theory and School Experience. The education component may run concurrently with the rest or be consecutive. It is usually offered in colleges of education, institutes of higher education and polytechnics. It can be either an initial or an in-service qualification.

DES   Department of Education and Science: The central department responsible for the general planning and organization of education in England. Northern Ireland and Scotland have separate organizations.

LEA   Local education authority: Detailed planning and organization is the responsibility of local education departments. In more rural areas they will deal with a whole county, but metropolitan counties are divided into districts for educational administration.

MA and MEd   Master of Arts, and Master of Education Degrees: The most usual higher degrees in education in the United Kingdom, they can be awarded for in-service research or course work, part-time or full-time.

OU   Open University: A 'distance' teaching organization operating through postal, television and radio programmes, plus local tutorials and short courses and awarding its own degrees.

SC   Schools Council: A centrally funded body which works through professional committees in the fields of curriculum and examining, innovation and evaluation.

TC   Teachers' centre: A building, usually provided by the LEA, which contains accommodation for teachers' meetings, libraries and general resources. If used for more extensive in-service activities it may be referred to as a 'professional centre', and often has a local title, as in LTC = Liverpool Teachers' Centre. It may include advisory headquarters or be based in a college of education.

TT   Teacher tutor: A teacher usually with special responsibility for the guidance and professional development of new teachers in their probationary (first) year in school. May be referred to as a 'professional tutor' and is a potential focus for school-based in-service activities.

PART ONE
PRINCIPLES AND EXPERIENCE

Chapter One

AIMS AND METHODS

(a)   General Aims and Ideas

There is a lot of in-service work for teachers going on. Investment in
it seems to be increasing. Much of this work is a development of local
and well-tried courses intended to improve teachers' classroom effectiveness or of regional provision of award-bearing courses. These aim
generally at extending minds as well as knowledge and turning the results
back into practice. The growth of the former reflects the increasing concern and involvement of local authorities in the field, especially through
the activities of their advisers, and the latter is possibly a consequence
of this as well as an increased recognition of a need for qualifications.
In a time of falling rolls and greater emphasis upon staff development both
activities become more important.

Another major area, an innovation in itself, is in-service work which seeks
to bring about desired changes and innovation in school or college organization and curriculum, while all the time teachers and advisers are trying
to introduce new methods or subjects into in-service programmes, some
authority-, and some school-based. The field is therefore wide and its
aims are complex, and varied, but as investment in it both of time and
money grow, and as more individuals' professional futures become dependent
upon it, so too does the need to examine whether it is worthwhile.

Evaluation is a wider and probably less threatening term than either assessment or examination, but perhaps carries with it too much of an implication
of 'value for money' or 'accountability' for comfort. It is a pity that
'examination' is so often taken in a limited sense, because to examine something we are doing and see whether it is worthwhile is a commonsense procedure, one that we all carry out and see a need for. There is indeed a
need to examine, at every stage, what goes on in in-service work and to
have the results passed on to those responsible - in fact to everyone concerned - so that this important work can be improved and made as effective
as possible. The examination is of courses and procedures and should not
seem sinister to individuals. It is a little unfortunate that this simple
idea of examining what we (organizers, teachers and students on courses

together) are doing should have accumulated the mystique which now tends to surround the term 'evaluation', but this is the sort of thing which 'education' does to words.

Evaluation has become a field of debate, accumulating disagreements about concepts, definitions and ideologies. It is a lively field and many of its debated methods and approaches are first summarized and later illu- strated in this book, but a first point to be made is that it is not a matter for experts but for practitioners - for all those involved in the work. It means essentially finding out what is being done, on, say a course; what people think of it; what its results are (planned or unplanned); and reporting all these fairly, and in such a way that the report is for the good of education. All teachers therefore need to know what evaluation is about and to understand their part in examining and improving what is being done for their professional development, as well as the good of their pupils. It is as integral to in-service provision as it should be to school organization and it is this which makes it both a proper subject of study for teachers and a way to improve effectiveness. There is a place for experts in evaluation, but I suggest that their role should be to be called in as skilled tradesmen who know the range of techniques and approaches which can be applied to a given situation, or as consultants who can advise on methods. It is course leaders and members who produce the evaluation even if someone else writes it up.

A strong case can be made out for saying that the general idea of evalua- tion as a commonsense examination of what is being done in any course or programme should be part of all our in-service work. The finding of the right questions to ask is itself a difficult and valuable in-service activity. But, since on any large scale it must be in competition for time and money, evaluation must justify itself and define its own aims and roles. Some of the main ones which will be dealt with in turn are:

1. To monitor and assess the progress of innovation.
2. To examine with some degree of objectivity the relative values of current provision and methods in terms of both process and product.
3. To register and recommend successful practices and approaches.
4. To record and disseminate findings so as to bring about a levelling up and a next generation of effective practice and fruitful concepts.

1.   The management of innovation in education has been studied fairly intensively (see, for example, Bolam, 1975) and the evaluation of both the processes and products of that innovation are part of the management pro- gramme. On the major level, then, this is an example of evaluation as a management tool, but at each and every other level it becomes part of all the activities involved, so that it concerns and affects not just the gate- keepers or controllers of the innovation at that level, but everyone whom the enterprise touches. It becomes more than a fact-finding operation from a distance, rather a series of examples of small-scale participatory studies all contributing to the total picture. It not only provides reports on progress but shapes that progress, involves the teachers affected by it and becomes part of the results and products of the innovation.

A major example which illustrates this combination of approaches in this decade has been the introduction of induction schemes for new entrants to teaching. This, from one point of view, is not true in-service training but more of a bridge between initial training and professional development (from another view, of course, it can be seen as the introductory stage of in-service work), but it is work with teachers on the job through courses, day-release, school-based programmes and tutorial sessions. Its evaluation was a matter of applying and developing the techniques appropriate to in-service work and examples from it are therefore given later to illustrate the management of a large-scale evaluation, as well as more intimate work with teachers who had school needs as their focus.

The pilot study was planned to cover some five authorities, each of which was to commission its own independent evaluation, with a central team based in Bristol to coordinate their activities and disseminate results. In the event only two local authorities and some non-official schemes were started, but the scale and the cost of such an evaluation were shown to be considerable, and must be from now on major factors in planning any national pilot project. The evaluation team (the local evaluators plus the Bristol team) met regularly to plan programmes and conferences, agree work divisions and design and process questionnaires. Each local evaluator produced a report outlining both how the scheme developed and some final (summative) comments (McCabe, 1978; Davis, 1979) while the final report came from Bristol (Bolam, 1979). Had there been enough finance available for the launching of the national scheme it would not have waited for the final or near-final report stages but would have got under way on the evidence of the first year or two. For this reason descriptions and assessments of successful processes and approaches were what were mostly wanted from the evaluators until the final summative stage when they could review the whole programme. Reliance had to be placed largely on 'informed professional opinion', sampled as carefully as possible, and little assessment involving 'measurement' was possible. Apart from the major national questionnaires and sets of interviews the task for each evaluator became one of gaining the confidence of local teachers, lecturers and advisers while organizing individual series of evaluations of courses, school-based work and day-release activities. All these were reported on locally, and so helped with the development of the project. The local aims became thus hardly distinguishable from the second general aim - to examine with some degree of objectivity the relative values of current provision and methods in terms of both process and product.

2. Clearly, if the same job can be done more economically by one course rather than another, then someone should discover this and report on it; but how do you define 'the same job' and how far should you allow for personal involvement? At a practical extreme, for instance, an adviser with an education authority organizes a course for teachers of his subject in his own area. He knows them all fairly well, can judge and distinguish between their needs and their wants - there are thousands of these courses every year. The best and only practicable way to assess if they are worthwhile seems to be to rely on the judgement of the individuals concerned - but is this enough? How far should one insist on formal consultations with students being carried out and reported upon - possibly after further discussions with all participants? How objective should the process be? Would

there be a net gain? The emphasis is on the problem of interpreting the phrase 'with some degree of objectivity' and at the same time the danger of leaving it out. At a theoretical extreme how far should evaluation be objective? Obviously someone, at some point, has to reach a decision as to the relative value of the course or programme - but need this be the evaluator? Is it possible for the evaluator to be a gatherer of evidence only? I suggest not, because otherwise his report would be unmanageable and unreadable. He has to choose, probably in consultation with tutors and teachers, what evidence to collect, so a subjective element has entered already at this point and becomes still greater when it comes to deciding what to put into a report and what recommendations to make or conclusions to draw. Even if he is merely an administrator of standardized measures or questionnaires, the evaluator's judgement is involved from first to last, so this is as close to objectivity as he can get.

There is a school of thought which would confine evaluation to this 'near objectivity' and to the observation of 'behavioural outcomes'. Taken to its limit this would involve measuring pupils' performance before their teachers went on the course and then again after a suitable interval following their return, to see whether there was a change in their performance which reflected the aims of the course. All results would be quantified in terms of cost-effectiveness. Comment and opinion would be irrelevant. So few educational aims are measurable in these terms, however, and the precise direction of desired change is so hard to identify, that however desirable this 'hard' approach may seem it is neither humanly nor philosophically possible. Many evaluators do tend to the view that one should use as many 'hard' measures as prove practicable and so be as objective as possible, with statistical tests to demonstrate relationships and their significances, or at least quotable numbers or percentages at the end of the exericse.

This school of course reflects one of the main approaches to educational research in general, and its opposite is the 'soft' school, which goes to the other extreme and relies upon sensitive studies of individuals and processes, involving the individuals fully in discussions about what is to be considered and how it should be reported; that is, participation is made as complete as possible, avoiding anything more objective than questionnaire data. Wilson (1979) gives a fresh discussion of the problems raised by the contrasting approaches, using as examples, among others, the cases of educational research and examinations. He labels the extremes of the points of views as the 'behaviourist fantasy' and the 'relativist fantasy'. His thesis applies equally to evaluation and just as in examinations the most practical recommendation is to use as valid as possible a mixture of forms of examination, so in evaluation to use a justifiable variety of techniques is probably the wisest course. Those commissioning evaluation studies, however, often have their own fantasies on the subject, so that evaluators and course members together may find that they have to negotiate a reasonable and acceptable series of approaches.

Opportunities to set up classical research situations of experimental versus control groups would be welcome in in-service evaluations, but they occur only rarely, partly because courses and programmes cannot usually be arranged that way (but see Bradley and Eggleston, 1977), and partly because so many variables cannot be controlled. Comparisons between different courses and course outcomes must be made with caution for the same reasons, and also because 'outcomes' are so hard to classify in precise terms and depend so much on the ground in which the seed is planted. As one example of difficulty: course results depend very much on the sort of school to which the course member returns; for another: different course organizations or methods often result in the terms used in attitude scales or question-naires being interpreted differently. This is not to say that cautious comparisons are not possible or desirable, but that they are not to be expected as normal evaluation design.

The range of techniques to be applied will depend upon the nature of the course to be dealt with. Courses leading to qualifications generally in-corporate their own accountability procedure through having external asses-sors to moderate methods and standards; end-of-course questionnaires and discussions, together with the evidence of the acceptability of the quali-fication in the job market, add further dimensions. Results and develop-ments observed in schools are the advisers' guides to the effectiveness of local authority courses, but the use of questionnaires (possibly anony-mous) and bringing in a colleague to comment on the occasional course give further opportunities to assess whether needs are really being met; some assessment of course members' expectations before the course, and a com-parison between these and (a) the course leaders aims, and (b) what they claim to have learned afterwards, can also be salutary procedures.

What methods are acceptable will usually have to be negotiated with course members, often with professional associations or local education authorities, and work to be done in schools must be approved by headteachers. Anything tending towards the personality area is unlikely to be acceptable to all individuals, whilst any measure which could be interpreted as being one of professional competence in school is unlikely to be acceptable at all.

Responses to questionnaires and attitude scales tend to be polite and to favour the course tutors. The evaluator is fair game for criticism by anyone. In this country parents are perhaps not consulted as much as they should be - in some countries they attend and are the keenest critics of in-service courses for teachers. A discussion of approaches to the evalu-ation of short courses of a sub-regional type, together with an example, is given at the end of this chapter.

3.   The evaluation aim and methods discussed in the last section tended to be concerned with comparisons and competition between courses, but this is not the aspect of evaluation which is the most useful, nor the most wanted even by management. Evaluation is most useful when it is concerned with stimulating interest in improving in-service courses or programmes and with finding out what are the best ways to organize and run them. Product and summative evaluations are needed to validate courses, but process and for-mative operations as discussed by Bolam in Chapter Three are the more positive and productive parts of the work.

The third general aim therefore stresses the need for evaluation to be a positive affair, emphasizing the good and recommendable. This also ensures that it will be as non-threatening as possible. What has gone wrong in any course is largely 'water under the bridge'. What is needed is to see which features contributed towards the attainment of the aims of the course, what aims and outcomes were attained (designedly or not), what approaches or methods can be confidently recommended for future courses or further parts of the programme. Features to be avoided in future can usually be indicated generally and briefly.

For questionnaires to be acceptable it is advisable to couch them in terms which emphasise this aim...'Would you recommend that this (lecture, workshop session, day's visit, week's course) be included as part of the programme of a similar course next year?' is the sort of style which encourages respondents to think positively and seems to ensure as thoughtful or reliable an answer as can be expected from this medium of consultation. Attitude measures can, being more general, include both 'for' and 'against' statements but, shifts or changes are here more significant, rather than the immediate level of response.

4. Finally and yet more positively I suggest that a main aim of carrying out and communicating the results of evaluation is to prevent each successive generation from having to re-invent the wheel. Much of the educational research carried out here or elsewhere may not have been very good or useful but, even when it has been both, all too often it has had no effect because there has been no effective body to which it could be reported, no organization which could arrange for its findings to be tested further or to be put into practice. In-service education is a practical and intensive activity run by organizing bodies on at least local scale. It therefore has the machinery to put into effect the results of evaluation and so lift the level of in-service teaching - and also of its evaluation - continuously.

We all have to try ideas for ourselves and learn from our own mistakes, in teaching as in anything else, but, when so much is already being taught well and so many courses and programmes are being organized effectively, information and guidance about successful methods should be available within each local area. It could also be accumulated and disseminated more widely on regional levels. Taylor in the next chapter suggests that there is a need for more meetings and discussions between evaluators. More meetings between organizing bodies to promote the results of evaluation would be at least equally valuable.

After looking at something of the aims and approaches, it is possible to appreciate the skills and techniques required to undertake evaluations. Some are skills of the psychological and sociological technician - knowledge of sampling techniques, the ability to select and administer standardized tests of ability or achievement, experience in drawing up and using attitude measures, practice in interviewing and in constructing questionnaires, for instance. How much of any of these is needed depends upon the form of the evaluation to be undertaken. Often a technical consultant can do what is required, but most of these techniques are available from standard texts or courses, and the ready availability of computers makes them much less arduous than they once were. An evaluation team needs access to such skills; some teachers should be expert in their application; all teachers would be better off with an intelligent knowledge of their uses and limitations.

A second set of necessary skills, referred to by Bolam, is that of design-ing and negotiating with all those involved, whether course providers or members, an acceptable methodology. These skills are more likely to be both personal and learned through assisting in evaluations than learned from texts, but the putting-together and presenting of an acceptable package of practicable procedures, together with the theory that underlies them, requires a fairly sophisticated appreciation of what evaluation is about. The negotiation is part of the evaluation and is the first oppor-tunity for participation and involvement which course members get. It can be, therefore, a useful part of the programme. The methodology of evaluation must influence the course and if well chosen can assist it greatly. The form of the evaluation must clearly be in keeping with the aims of the course - it would be unfortunate if the aim of the course were the group exploration of individual insights in a developing and thera-peutic way, while the evaluator was a victim of the behaviourist fantasy, so that the message of the evaluation was that the course was wrong and valueless. Some of the later examples indicate how the evaluation can promote and enhance a suitable course.

Because of the interaction between evaluation and course content and between evaluation and course members it is difficult at times to distinguish between carrying out an evaluation and teaching evaluation. The best way to learn about evaluation is to be part of one, and conversely, to parti-cipate in one which is properly conducted is an educating experience which forms attitudes to evaluation in the widest sense and can lead to new ways of looking at our work as teachers and assessors, particularly in relation-ships and co-operation with colleagues and students. It is not claimed that all evaluations have this effect but it may be an aim to work towards.

The skill which has not been mentioned so far but which runs through all the others is the one which I would call 'interpretation'. Judgement is involved, as we have seen, but where it really matters it becomes part of interpretation. First of all it is not entirely correct to say that the collecting of objective evidence in a clean and orderly way is simply a matter of technique, because the selection of that evidence and its inter-pretation are the skilled parts of the task; but, more fundamentally, the evaluator must also be an interpreter of human transaction in Hudson's sense (Hudson, 1972). Hudson's Law of Selective Attention to Data could be a landmark for all evaluators, but here we concentrate on a modified form of his codicil to it: 'The evaluator should envisage his work as a process wherein one person becomes acquainted with others' ('psychologist' in the original).

One aspect of this metaphor which Hudson mentions as particularly apt is the removal from the psychologist of his: 'God-like exemption from sub-jectivity of judgement. It accepts the practical constraints of working with other people...It places centrally what belongs centrally - the act of making sense; and it does so without diminishing the significance of behaviour either as evidence, or as part of what this act of making sense seeks to encompass or explain.' At this stage the weight of (Hudson, 1972, pp.162-4) the metaphor is interpretative and it seems to me that the key educational role of the evaluator is that of being an interpreter, with all that that concept involves.

The task of the average evaluator on the average bread-and-butter job is
simpler and more common-sense (after allowing for fantasies) than this
discussion may suggest, but the responsibilities can be heavy and having
gone so far it may be as well to ask one further question: How far should
the evaluator see himself as a psychotherapist? Two references used here
give indications in this direction. Keast and Carr, (1979) describe the
role of the evaluator of school-based work as having this responsibility
in the sense of guiding the new development towards its fullest flowering.
In this sense the description does hold and could be taken as the aim of
the interpretative activity already described. Wilson (1979) calls for
further work on his theme of Fantasy and Common-sense in Education in
which 'we cannot get very far without many more professional psychotherapists'.
Since so much of what he discusses applies to evaluation the same idea could
be developed here - perhaps 'a small and close-knit team of philosophers
and psychotherapists' could reform both the questions to be answered and
the methods to be used in the field.

Both of these ideas, however, come together with others to stimulate
parallels between the tasks of an evaluator working closely with a group -
see later examples - and that of a psychotherapist. There are obviously
dangers in taking the parallel too far or in an evaluator getting illusions
that he really is a psychotherapist, but as a guide to procedure and
behaviour it may be safer than the extremes of fantasy. It invites further exploration.

This chapter so far has introduced terms, ideas and matters of debate
which are developed and illustrated in subsequent chapters. There they
are discussed in relation to the contexts in which they have been used.
As a first example and to apply the ideas already raised to a firm base
the rest of the chapter discusses them in relation to the evaluation of
short courses.

Introduction and Aims

The commonest form of in-service education and training for teachers is the short course. Advisers and teachers invest significant amounts of their time in them, local authorities as well as the Department of Education and Science (DES) pay for their running, and the courses themselves are very much a part of most teachers' professional development. This section therefore draws together some ideas about the evaluation of such courses in the form of a brief guide put together with the interests of short course organizers or committees in mind.

Evaluation and its aims have so far been discussed in general terms. In more detail the aims of short course evaluation, even where it is simply carried out by the organizer or co-ordinator responsible for the activity, should be, I suggest, fivefold.

1. To provide a description of what happened. This seems perhaps unnecessary but if a course is to be repeated or improved upon such a record is needed. The programme is rarely adhered to and it is often variations from the intended pattern or special physical or other circumstances which lead to improved effectiveness.

2. To assess the educational value of the course. There are two aspects to this and both require the valuable activity of standing back from involvement with the subject and the students. The more practical-seeming side is that of looking at the outcomes and results of the course and assessing whether they justify the effort and money involved, but as well as this obvious activity some attempt has to be made to tackle the important area of defining what questions the content of the course was intended to answer and what its educational objectives (not necessarily in a behavioural sense) might be. The remaining three aims come from such an examination of evaluation itself.

3. To give opportunities to and to accustom both teachers who are tutors on the courses, and teachers who are their students, to open up what they are doing to each other without feeling threatened. This simple aim could help to show that criticism should not be a negative activity and that the examination and evaluation of what one is doing in teaching are helpful and important.

4. To improve future courses by identifying those techniques, approaches and organizational details which have been proved to be effective. There may on occasion be features which all concerned agree should be noted 'Never Again' as warnings to future organizers, but evaluation is not intended to be a fault-finding or noting activity.

5. There is some agreement that in planning a piece of teaching, whether it be a lesson, a series of lessons or a course, four items should be linked inextricably: Objectives, Content, Method and Evaluation, with all that this pattern involves. Short courses for teachers are no exception. The aim and place of evaluation must be much the same as they are in any other teaching.

Notes for Committee Discussion

SPONSORS

It is assumed that everyone involved in providing or attending courses needs reassurance that their efforts are worthwhile. A committee made up largely of senior advisers and teachers is the sort of body which usually decides which of the many courses suggested will go into the coming year's programme. This committee therefore must commission and provide for course evaluation if it is to work at more than the simplest level.

REPORTS FOR WHOM

This committee would also seem to be the body to which evaluation reports should be presented, but such reports are of interest and importance also to those who attend the courses (whom I shall refer to as students) to those who teach on and lead the courses ('tutors') and to other teachers and administrators. It is essential to decide to whom the reports should be available, since this may determine both the nature of the evaluation and the form of report adopted.

NON-THREATENING

The ways in which the process of evaluation as well as its aims are presented to the tutors and students affect its acceptability. It must not be seen in any way as a threat, but as a co-operative, helpful, positive affair. Experience of being part of a careful and thoughtful evaluation is a valuable part of teachers' professional development and is the best way to learn to overcome fears and develop appropriate skills.

SOME GENERAL CONSIDERATIONS

(i) Policy - what proportion of courses should be subjected to what degree of evaluation?

(ii) Should it be predominently large-scale (e.g. general questionnaires to all), or smaller scale (e.g. intensive discussions with small samples)?

(iii) How much of the money allowed for a course should go on evaluation?

(iv) Are final discussions and feed-back questionnaires already included in each course programme?

(v) Who should carry out the evaluation?

THE ARMOURY

A very good evaluation checklist, based upon school-focused arrangements, is given in the pamphlet *Making INSET work* (Great Britain, DES, 1978). Some possible techniques for general use, however, are:

> participant observer - continuous or intermittent
> reports by course tutors
> questionnaires at stages of course - and some weeks after its close
> final (or intermediate) evaluation discussions
> records of continuing attendance
> attitude scales
> collection of hoped-for objectives at the start and comparison with
>   outcomes at the end (tutors and/or student)
> views, assessments, of school i.e. of the students' colleagues, heads?
> testing of pupils before and after
> observation of pupils/classes before and after
> comparison of teacher-students statements/essays before and after
> testing of teacher-students before and after
> examination at end of the course
> records of students' progress/development through the course.

OBJECTIVES AND TECHNIQUES

The ultimate aim of and the real justification for INSET is the benefit of pupils in school. Ideally improvements in their welfare or performance are what should be looked for as the outcomes of a course. As a rule it is not possible to either identify or assess the extent of such outcomes so we have to fall back on secondary evidence...changes in students' attitudes or performance...or more usually tertiary sources which rely on the students' and their colleagues' informed professional opinions about the course, not always explicitly expressed, obtained mostly through questionnaires. According to the situation, appropriate techniques can be selected to effect a reasonably objective evaluation.

Introducing an evaluator who is involved in the course, probably as a participant observer, adds another dimension altogether. Such an evaluator affects the progress of the course but can draw together and describe aspects of the programme and students' reactions which are otherwise missed completely and give a quite different quality and value to the evaluation.

MINIMAL FEEDBACK

It may be felt that for every course there should be at least a minimal record kept, consisting of a brief objective account of the course programme, an attendance register and the results of a final 'course assessment' questionnaire, possibly supplemented by notes of a final discussion. The supplying of this record could be part of the task of the course leader and its evidence referred to in annual reviews.

STANDARD GENERAL REPORTS

Where an evaluator is invited to report generally on a course, then experience, particularly with induction courses, has shown that four components are usually needed if the report is to be acceptable. These are:

1. A description of the aims, physical circumstances and programme of the course together with the groupings and methods which resulted and something about their outcomes;

2. Notes made and opinions expressed by the course tutors and leaders;

3. Some summary of opinions expressed by course members - at the lowest level as a response to a questionnaire;

4. An introduction, a conclusion and a structure given to the whole by the evaluator.

The third of these items is probably the hardest to present in a report, even allowing for the difficult choice of the appropriate modes of consultation, since the evaluator has to decide how to combine them fairly, meaningfully and interestingly. He finds himself with material which may on average express one set of opinions, but taking its extremes or forms of distribution may give a different impression, with his most quotable conversations or comments distinctly biassed and possibly all from one type of respondent; and he knows that one piece of criticism will be picked up where ten more favourable comments can apparently be overlooked by those for whom the report is intended.

The description of the course and its development becomes of much greater value if it is produced by a participant observer who will include significant material which is more subjective, individual and important, but less tangible. If it is desired to introduce more of the approaches usually referred to as 'democratic' then the balance of the report will be changed considerably and naturally.

PRACTICAL PROPOSALS FOR A SUB-REGIONAL COMMITTEE RESPONSIBLE FOR SHORT COURSES

1. All course leaders should give the committee secretary, on the completion of their course, a minimal report of the type referred to earlier unless an outside evaluation is commissioned.

2. Where a course seems of special significance (say three in each year) an individual not already involved should be invited to produce a standard general report on the lines already described but with such extensions, e.g. later follow-up questionnaires or interviews, as seem appropriate. This need not involve close contact with the course.

3. When a course appears particularly innovatory (perhaps one each year) then a participant observer type of evaluation could be commissioned.

4. Whenever evaluation can be made an integral part of a course - as both process and product, teaching method and valuable outcome - this should be encouraged.

WHO SHOULD DO IT?

It is well for an outside evaluator to be someone experienced in course work, and in evaluation (but not necessarily in the subject of the course), who gets on with the course leader. Since carrying out an evaluation is a valuable experience, having a teacher-assistant can be valuable for both. It might help if they were to discuss their evaluation proposals and progress with an evaluation consultant.

POSSIBLE COST

Minimal evaluation should involve no extra cost

Standard general report : a small basic fee - but some secretarial help would be needed.

Participant observer evaluation : a fee not far short of that of a teacher on the course.

ONE EXAMPLE

As a result of discussing the above notes with one sub-regional committee a pattern for evaluating short courses in the following year was agreed upon. This included a 'participant observer' evaluation of a one-week residential course planned for primary school teachers drawn from seven local authorities and with a form of programme rather different from the normal. The evaluation activities planned may be a useful example of what can be done.

(Two notes will indicate the background to such an evaluation::

1. A participant observer procedure was administratively and economically easier to arrange than something less ambitious because the evaluator could be included in the staffing lists and estimates.

2. There was an element of challenge in the commission. 'You have told us that short-course evaluation may be important and helpful. While we accept that it is, show us what you can do in this case.'

Individuals at this stage do have to be convinced that formal evaluation of what they do is worth the trouble. I use the term 'formal' here to indicate an evaluation which is something more than what conscientious course leaders always carry out - not only a personal and implicit assessment of worthwhileness, but rather one which is explicit and could be used to justify course procedures and values to say, a funding organization or parents. The very fact that this particular course is not an example which this evaluator would have chosen for himself also makes it a characteristic task for evaluation - an evaluator cannot choose what needs evaluating).

Coming into the field soon after the course programme was planned the evaluator met the organizer (course leader) to discuss what would be involved and be informed about aims, arrangements and what had happened so far - had she been able to appoint the course tutors she wanted, for instance. Following this the evaluator met key tutors and then attended the final programme planning meeting, emphasizing throughout that evaluation is not something being done to anyone but a co-operative activity to assess the worthwhileness of what is planned for the future good of education.

A sample of eight applicants to attend the course was selected and the applicants were visited in their schools to find out why they had applied and what their expectations were. About the same time the evaluator joined the course team for a preliminary visit to the course venue, planned an initial questionnaire and, more roughly, brought together ideas for a short attitude measure to suit what he had found about those who would attend.

During the course, having been introduced as a (non-threatening) evaluator he was able to move between groups, joining in their activities and their social life in the evenings, discussing impressions as well as taking part in tutors' evening assessment sessions.

A questionnaire supplemented the final evaluation and review discussion periods with everyone on the course and a final longer term follow-up was planned. Tutors and students were invited to send in reports and comments which would complete the picture.

A sample of six students were followed up into their schools a month or so later to see how far expectations had been fulfilled and whether anything had been changed. During the rest of the term local authority advisers called in to see further individuals in their own areas and reported on what they judged the effects of the course to be.

The effects of such a programme might well take more than three months to show themselves significantly but for practical purposes the main evaluation was stopped at that point. A report was drawn up and discussed with the organizer and her colleagues before putting it into its final form for submission to the committee which commissioned the evaluation.

That the course was changed by the inclusion of the evaluator is undeniable. That the extra dimension that was added improved its effectiveness or at least widened its significance and influence and will help future planning is a matter for yet further evaluation.

Chapter Two

A REVIEW OF SOME IN-SERVICE EVALUATION STUDIES UNDERTAKEN IN THE UK

Peter Taylor, University of Bristol

The evaluation of in-service activities is of course not new, for it has been going on for years though on an ad hoc basis, and using some limited but nevertheless sometimes helpful techniques. For example, based upon the results of a review which I have undertaken for the DES, it would appear that the vast majority of evaluation attempts undertaken in the United Kingdom so far have used one or more of the following for the collection of data:-

1. The distribution of questionnaires to teacher participants either during or at the end of an activity, or both, often asking them to rate various aspects of a course or programme of activities.

2. Examination and continuous assessment techniques, which are particularly applicable in the case of award-bearing programmes.

3. Informal subjective assessment of classroom effect by local authority advisory staff, and to a lesser extent by college and university tutors and others, who regularly visit schools.

4. Reports from course organizers and tutors.

5. Evaluation conferences or meetings.

6. Occasionally, the appointment of part-time or full-time evaluators using more sophisticated techniques.

However, the extent of even these attempts has been limited and the time has arrived, especially in view of the limited resources which are going to be available for INSET, when more vigorous systematic evaluation studies should be undertaken, which yield additional kinds of information and which are potentially more accurate and valid.

The findings of the review are particularly encouraging in this respect, in that they indicate that a substantial number of in-service providing agencies appear to accept the necessity for more systematic studies. Other encouraging developments include: some increase in such studies during the last four to five years; a recent seminar organized by the Society for Research into Higher Education relating to the evaluation of new BEd degree courses; another organized by the Committee for Research into Teacher Education on research into in-service teacher education; the introduction of Evaluation Newsletter by the same body; a conference organized by the Cambridge Institute of Education relating to the evaluation of courses and conferences.

In undertaking the review, I attempted to locate any promising evaluation studies, principally from a methodology point of view. Some of them are being reported on elsewhere in this book, and others will be commented on here. Some, which describe the organization of evaluation in larger institutions, are dealt with in more detail than the rest.

The Evaluation of teacher education – the range of procedures in Didsbury College

Prior to reorganization, as a result of recent developments in teacher education in the United Kingdom, Didsbury College of Education had its initial and in-service award-bearing teacher education courses validated by Manchester University. However, that link has now ceased, the College is now part of Manchester Polytechnic, and its courses are being validated by the Council for National Academic Awards.

From the outset of this new era, the College decided that it should evaluate its new teacher education courses, namely, the Post-graduate Certificate in Education, initial BEd and two in-service BEd degree courses. To do this it established an evaluation team in 1974, consisting of an Adviser on Evaluation (with half-time release from teaching duties for this purpose), assisted by a full-time Evaluation Research Assistant, and part-time Clerical Assistant, both now funded by the Social Science Research Council. The College also has an Evaluation Committee (set up in 1975 as a new standing committee of the Academic Board) consisting of representatives from course committees, lecturers and students, which suggests an evaluation programme for each academic year. This programme incorporates suggestions from course committees, departments and the Students' Union, so that there is maximum participation in drawing up a programme from students, lecturers and course managers.

In evaluating these four courses the College has also been anxious to devise and mount studies in varied evaluation techniques which can eventually be institutionalized, i.e. taken over by course teams as regular evaluation procedures in order to improve teaching and learning, and to contribute to the educational and intellectual development of the College and its teachers. The evaluation programme is, therefore, concerned with the development of evaluation procedures as well as evaluation findings.

All documentation on procedures is made widely available throughout the College so that the process can be seen by those involved to be 'open' and 'participatory'. Once the feedback material has been processed, analyses go in the first instance back to lecturers for their response, before the 'package' of procedures, analyses and response is forwarded in summary form to the Academic Board.

The College does not claim to provide a complete evaluation service but has opted for a selective and shifting focus from one year to the next. By July 1976, the following evaluation activities had been attempted:-

Initial BEd

1. Foundation studies, using tutors' self evaluation schedules.

2. Student routes through courses - analysis of student records and interviews.

3. Professional studies - questionnaires to students, tutors and teachers in associated schools. Collated records of evaluation meetings.

4. Student workloads - questionnaires.

5. Rationale and practice in degree as a whole - interviews, participant observation, portrayal evaluation questionnaires.

Postgraduate Certificate in Education

1. Student expectations of course - questionnaires.

2. Student and tutor feedback at selected points - questionnaires.

3. Schools' responses to school experience - meetings.

4. Former students' perceptions of course in relation to probationary year - diaries and questionnaires.

In-service BEd

1. Student and tutor feedback at selected points - questionnaires and interviews.

In-service BEd (Social Handicap)

1. The tutorial session as a means of course evaluation - participant observation.

Although it is still in its early stages, a number of points from this study deserve noting. It appears to be a fairly wide ranging evaluation study, especially as far as the first two programmes are concerned. It is an example of an internal evaluation which has used a variety of instruments, and appears to have been guided by the 'illuminative' model originating from Parlett and Hamilton (1972). The Evaluation Committee is an innovation which has helped to give support to the evaluation team. By going to considerable lengths to make the evaluation 'open and participatory', it has also attempted to overcome staff hostility and reluctance to participate, although it has by no means overcome this. Its second main purpose, i.e. to produce evaluation techniques which can be taken over by course teams and individuals, is promising, although it is too early yet to estimate its success. As an internal study it might be accused of lacking credibility, but in this case the appointment of a very able evaluation officer does to some extent counteract that criticism. It has already resulted in some modifications to the courses.

*A 'Student Feedback' service in a Polytechnic (North East
London (NELP)*

The Student Feedback Project which commenced in 1973 at North East London
Polytechnic (which provides both initial and in-service teacher education
courses) examines and develops methods of evaluating teaching and courses,
offering help and advice to members of staff who wish to evaluate their
course programmes, and their teaching, in terms of students' opinions.
The service, which is staffed by a small number of academics with supporting secretarial assistance, may be used either by individual lecturers or
by course operation groups at NELP.

Individual teachers can take advantage of the service by requesting copies
of the Student Feedback Questionnaire. This is a teaching evaluation
questionnaire, consisting of twenty-three statements related chiefly to
large class and lecture methods of teaching. Students are asked to rate
the lecturer on each of the statements and to rate the statements themselves for importance. The completed questionnaire may then be sent back
to the Project for analysis, or alternatively a teacher may analyse the
results himself or by using a computer programme available for the purpose,
and from the results he may make changes to his teaching. During 1974/5
and 1975/6 over one hundred lecturers used the questionnaire. A set of
notes relating to the analysis and interpretation of the results are
returned with summaries of results.

In addition to the standard questionnaire, it is now planned to offer a
wider service to academic staff. For example, for those staff who find the
standard questionnaire inappropriate, an item bank of statements covering
a wide range of teaching skills has been completed. Staff may select items
from the list, and these will be prepared as a questionnaire. This questionnaire can then be used in exactly the same way as the standard questionnaire,
and when returned to the Feedback Project will be analysed as before. In
addition, the Project Team are also prepared to offer group discussions
aimed at identifying strengths and weaknesses of a course as perceived by
students; individual interviews with individual students and/or staff,
either to obtain an overall evaluation of the course or of specific aspects
of it; and observation of lecturers/classes either by a member of the Project or a lecturer outside NELP.

Most institutions of higher education in the United Kingdom would probably
agree that at the moment they could not provide the resources needed for
a similar project to this. However, given that any significant increase
in the evaluation of teacher education courses and other courses of higher
education will have to be undertaken by providing agencies and tutors themselves, this would seem to be one approach for those who have the resources.
It provides a service which makes few demands upon tutors themselves, and
it can be confidential. However, until recently, it has been a very limited form of evaluation which has been primarily concerned with evaluating
teaching methods, including the presentation of course material, via
student reaction, and not with trying to assess the outcomes of courses on
the attitude and skills of students. This is no doubt partly due to the
difficulty in devising suitable instruments to measure such outcomes.
There is also nothing new in the techniques adopted, but the Polytechnic
is supporting one of the few attempts in the United Kingdom to provide a
feedback service for members of staff.

Another institution that has given attention to evaluation is Jordanhill College of Education, Glasgow, which is heavily involved in initial and in-service teacher training. Commencing in September 1975, the College offered a new four-term in-service sandwich course leading to the award of a Diploma in Educational Technology, the first of its kind in Scotland. The course is mainly taught on a 'distance-teaching' basis via base modules, i.e. instructional units which the College staff have themselves written and produced, and which are posted weekly to students. In addition, project work at base is undertaken when visits from tutors are made, and a limited amount of face-to-face teaching at College takes place.

From the beginning, the College recognized that a new, innovatory distance-teaching course such as this ought to be evaluated so that it could be modified or even rewritten, if necessary. The latter was seen to be par-ticularly important, as members of staff who had written the distance-teaching units had had little experience of this work before, although the draft modules had been piloted. As a result, the course team included a psychologist trained in techniques of assessment and evaluation. Apart from teaching these topics at the appropriate point in the course, she is concerned solely with evaluating the modular materials, and the teaching/learning methods employed in the face-to-face sessions at College.

Distance-teaching presents particular problems for the evaluator because of the difficulty in obtaining precise evidence about how base modules are used, and the degree of understanding associated with each part of a module. Performance on the base module exercises allows the College to make inferences about levels of difficulty, but the evidence is too generalized to act as a suitable guide when it comes to carrying out detailed revision. In evaluating the modules, therefore, the College uses the following in order to supplement information gathered from assess-ment:

1. Simple evaluation forms to obtain members' perceptions of difficulties. Students are asked to return these weekly.

2. Activity exercises built in at intervals throughout the modules. Responses to these exercises are written on 'print through sheets' and returned anonymously by course members as a means of providing evidence about their understanding of each section of the course.

3. Audio-cassette recordings, which students are invited to submit, giving their reactions to the modules in more detail than can be obtained in an evaluation form.

A further variety of techniques is employed to evaluate the College sessions (at each of which the evaluator is present), including struc-tured observation, specially constructed questionnaires, interviews and informal group discussions. In addition, information is collected from course team members, students' work, and the external examiner.

This is another internal evaluation study, which, like the two previous studies, is seen as on-going, and not as a 'one-off' operation. It is a fairly rigorous process which, like the Didsbury example, seems to have been based upon the illuminative model. It has also made a determined effort to cope with the difficulties involved in evaluating a distance-teaching course. The College has been fortunate in obtaining the help of a part-time evaluator who has some evaluation expertise, and in being able to make arrangements whereby the evaluator, who is normally a full-time teaching member of staff, can be excused from some of her teaching duties without a replacement being required. So far, the evaluation, perhaps for the reason mentioned in the last study, appears to have been primarily concerned with the course material and teaching methods, and not with assessing changes in skills and attitudes, although attempts are made through the assessment procedures to ascertain the extent of such changes. It is, however, a promising example of how we might set about evaluating a distance-teaching programme, given the necessary resources and small numbers of students.

The evaluation of a higher degree course in Sussex

A further useful, and seemingly straightforward, evaluation approach in connection with an award-bearing in-service course is that used at the University of Sussex School of Education in connection with the MA in Education (Curriculum Development in Higher Education). This course is designed to cater for the needs of staff with teaching experience in higher education, who are concerned with problems in curriculum development and evaluation. To date (1977), there have been two such courses and the following procedure and techniques have been used:

Formative evaluation

Tutorial feedback and course team discussions; formal feedback sessions, student projects and their assessment.

Summative evaluation

1. A detailed course description, which can be subjected to intrinsic evaluation by outside experts.

2. Student coursework, which can also be assessed by outside experts.

3. The reports of those involved in teaching the course, many of whom have long experience in advanced training.

4. The report of the external examiner.

5. Reports compiled by students just before the courses terminated.

6. Reports from former students after their first term back home.

7. Reports of interviews conducted by an independent agent with students approximately six months after the end of the course.

8. Report of a conference of staff and students from the first course held in April 1976, eight months after the end of the course.

9. Report of the way course material and experience have been used in the design of short courses.

33

10. Comments on the student reports by an independent referee of the students' own choice from within their own institution.

This again is a largely internal evaluation study which draws upon a variety of sources for information (some of which are integral parts of the courses), and it makes explicit strategies which are implicit in other programmes. It seems to be something that could quite easily be built into many courses.

So far this report has been concerned with examining some of the evaluation strategies used in connection with award-bearing programmes, but much British in-service provision takes the form of shorter activities, and it is the evaluation of these which probably presents the greatest problem because of their volume, diversity and lack of resources for evaluation purposes.

During the review, I came across few techniques available for this purpose which can be administered quickly and efficiently, other than those mentioned earlier. However, one approach, known as 'democratic evaluation', which has been influenced by the Ford Teaching Project (Elliott et al., 1974) has been used with success in some activities of this type, and therefore deserves attention. Briefly, democratic evaluation is an information service to the whole course or conference community about all aspects of the programme. Elliott's case study presented later in this book illustrates the approach. Thus, an evaluator or course study officer who is familiar with this form of evaluation seeks to represent a range of interests and acts as a broker dealing in the exchange of information between groups who want knowledge of each other. Basically, he adopts a 'triangulation' procedure and seeks to consider and compare three points of view about a programme; namely those of the organizers, the participants and the evaluator himself.

Further Studies from recent Literature

Lack of space prevents comment in any detail upon further studies, consequently brief details only are being given. Fuller information can be obtained from the relevant documents.

1. Course Feedback Programme: A short document produced by the Open University describing its original plans for a feedback service and what actually happens now. The University's Survey Research Unit mainly seeks feedback from students and tutors *via* the use of questionnaires, but course teams sometimes undertake more extensive studies.

2. Final Report of the Applied Education Project by D. McNamara, obtainable from University of Lancaster School of Education. The third section of the report describes the evaluation of a new initial teacher training course (subsequently offered in modified form as an in-service BEd) in which a control group and a variety of techniques, e.g. psychometric testing; structured interviews, questionnaires, and the Minnesota Teacher Attitude Inventory, were used. The evaluation was undertaken by a part-time evaluator with the assistance of the DES funds.

3. 'Innovative induction programmes: A case study of factors affecting the design, implementation and evaluation of induction programmes for beginning teachers in four LEAs by R. Bolam.

Unpublished PhD, University of Bristol. Part of the PhD. contains a useful analysis of the evaluation methodology (including its shortcomings) used in connection with this externally funded research project, which lasted for four years.

4. Evaluation Reports on the Progress of the Liverpool and Northumberland Pilot Schemes available from the Schools of Education of the Universities of Liverpool and Newcastle respectively.

5. An Induction Year Experiment, by H. Bradley and J.E. Eggleston. University of Nottingham, School of Education, 1976. This report describes the setting-up, evaluation and outcomes of a one-term pilot induction scheme involving first-year teachers from Lincolnshire, Derbyshire and Nottinghamshire. The main techniques used for gathering information in relation to the evaluation were the keeping of weekly diaries on three occasions during the term, and a job adjustment questionnaire administered three times. Reports from headmasters on different aspects of the scheme, and the recording of probationers' comments were also included. The diary and job adjustment questionnaire are well worth studying.

6. An Evaluation of an In-service Course for Professional Tutors 1973/4. Keswick Hall College of Education. A short document describing the evaluation of an experimental course for professional tutors. The small number on the course, the nature of the course itself, i.e. the fact that it was exploratory, the limited time and resources of the part-time evaluator and the experience of the evaluator in other areas of educational research resulted in 'traditional' methods of evaluation (the application of attitude, opinion and personality inventories at the start and end of the course for example) being rejected as inappropriate to this situation. Any forms of final testing, e.g. objective tests of knowledge and examinations, were also rejected as inappropriate.

Reliance was placed upon observation, discussions with and questioning of course members and tutors; consideration of course work; an examination of the course tutor's report; and reflection upon the process in which the teachers were involved. Thus the evaluation data was not 'hard' in the traditional sense.

7. The Ealing Pilot Induction Scheme 1973/4. Thomas Huxley College of Education. This document describes the setting-up of and evaluation of a pilot induction scheme in the London Borough of Ealing. It describes a constant evaluation process, which permitted a rigorous and controlled development of the induction programme. Diaries were kept by the inductees documenting the roles they had to play in the school-based situation; similarly professional tutors documented their school-based support roles. An almost 100 per cent observation of all centre-based activities was conducted by the Evaluation Officer, this being supplemented by the views and criticisms submitted at the end of each centre-based induction day by Course Tutors, Professional Tutors and inductees themselves. One-to-one interviews with inductees and their headteachers were also included. This was another time-consuming study which needed the support of a part-time evaluator.

9. 'A Study of Self Instructional Microteaching Systems' by
    E. Perrott in Educational Development International, 2, 1,
    pp. 19-25. This article describes a self-instructional
    training system based upon micro-teaching, which has pro-
    vided reliable evidence that the approach brings about
    significant and lasting changes in the performance of in-
    service teachers. A self-evaluation technique is involved.

10. Evaluating the 'Progress in Learning Science' dissemination.
    The 'Progress in Learning Science' project, which is being
    funded by the Schools Council, is concerned with helping teachers
    with the selection and guidance of science activities for chil-
    dren. As far as dissemination is concerned, however, since the
    project itself cannot run courses for more than a small number
    of teachers, the dissemination is being carried out using the
    usual channels of in-service work (see Elliott's later study).
    An important part of the project and a somewhat unusual develop-
    ment is that this dissemination process is being evaluated by a
    part-time evaluator, and, as the major part of the work is
    school based, part of the dissemination is to study in-service
    programmes actually operating in schools.

    The evaluation is largely adopting a case study approach using
    techniques of participation, observation, interviewing and
    triangulation. It aims to produce condensed field studies of a
    number of examples of the trial dissemination in action with a
    view to exploring and anticipating its outcomes. Such studies
    are made accessible as speedily as possible to the dissemination
    group and wider audiences in the hope of facilitating informed
    decision making. It is also intended to produce a final case
    study of the trial programme as an instance of a dissemination
    project in action. This study will draw upon the condensed
    field studies.

11. 'Some Personal and School Outcomes of In-Service Training'.
    Unpublished PhD, University of Reading, 1976. Euan Henderson,
    who has undertaken one of the very few higher degree research
    programmes in the UK relating to in-service evaluation, evaluated
    a substantial part-time course. A pre-course interview collected
    data on individuals and schools, while a second, loosely-structured,
    interview was found to be a far more precise evaluative tool than
    a questionnaire for examining a course's outcomes. Questionnaire
    ratings were obtained and it was possible to examine the validity
    of the ratings in terms of several external criteria. An attitude
    scale was also used.

    The combination of the three evaluative instruments (interviews,
    ratings and attitude scale) enabled detailed descriptions of each
    teacher's progress, or lack of progress, on the four course
    objectives to be compiled. Although this type of intensive approach
    to the evaluation of in-service training is very time-consuming, it
    seems likely that a greater understanding of the training process
    and of how its objectives emerge in personal and school behaviours
    can certainly come from studies along these lines.

Because INSET has no systematic evaluation tradition, whatever is done in the future in order to increase the number of reliable studies, will, in terms of methodology, to some extent be exploratory and experimental, at least in the initial stages. To conclude this section then, it might be helpful to indicate what we might endeavour to do to assist us in this task.

Some of the studies which I discovered during the review had obviously turned, rightly in my view, to the curriculum evaluation movement for guidance, both in terms of strategies and suitable instruments for the collection of data. The Schools Council work in this area is of particular interest and value (e.g. Schools Council Research Studies, 1973, in which Schools Council project evaluators relate aspects of their work). As a result, some of the curriculum evaluation models appear to have proved helpful. This prompts me to believe that it would be beneficial to evaluators of INSET if well-designed theoretical evaluation models could be made available.

Difficult as it is, there is also a need for us to give more attention to how we might try to ascertain more effectively the outcomes of in-service activities upon teachers attitudes, skills and ultimately classroom performance. Attitude tests are of course available, but their use could be extended. (The work of Bradley and Eggleston (1977), Henderson, Hoste and McCabe (1977), is relevant, and Henderson has also reviewed the literature of attitude change, (1976a).) In terms of assessing impact upon skills and classroom performance, however, the greatest developments, especially at initial training level, have been in the areas of micro-teaching and associated techniques and of interaction analysis, and further exploratory work in these fields would seem necessary.

As was noted earlier, however, because of lack of resources, any significant increase in the evaluation of in-service activities will probably have to be undertaken by providing agencies, i.e. colleges, universities, polytechnics, teachers' centres, LEAs and schools themselves. As some of the studies highlighted in this paper indicate, this is already happening, but for those agencies, especially teachers' centres, schools and LEAs, who do not have sufficient resources or expertise, help will need to be given, especially if their attempts are to be credible. I would suggest therefore, that something like the following should be explored:

1. The production of simple and straightforward evaluation instruments (perhaps in the form of evaluation packages) that can be used for formative and summative evaluation purposes, and which will be particularly applicable to the shorter activities which they tend to specialize in. Ideally these instruments should be easy to administer, should be based upon a common framework, and should use, within broad limits, common items, so that comparable area or regional data can be made. A major project will probably need to be funded in order to explore this possibility further.

2. Introductory evaluation courses, which are the equivalent of about three weeks in length, should be organized on a regional basis by those who have the expertise, e.g. universities and polytechnics, in order to supplement the instruments mentioned above. These

courses should be aimed at teachers' centre leaders, in-service organizing tutors, course tutors and others who are interested, and should contain a substantial workshop element, including the compiling of questionnaires, the conducting of interviews, taping and analysing in-service meetings, and writing meaningful evaluation reports. They should also be monitored.

Sufficient resources should also be made available for large-scale external evaluation studies of promising new approaches to INSET, particularly those which appear to have a significant part to play in future provision. The school-based or school-focused approach immediately comes to mind, and more information is needed to assist us in determining which activities are better undertaken on a part-time, as opposed to a full-time, basis, and vice versa.

Other steps that could be taken quickly, in my view, and which would be relatively cheap to arrange include:

1. Regional, national and international conferences to be arranged, perhaps by regional committees where they exist, or universities, the DES or the OECD, which would seek to stimulate the need for more evaluation, and to examine in some depth some of the major difficulties that confront evaluators of INSET, with a view to making recommendations to the appropriate bodies.

2. Opportunities to be made available so that those with a serious interest in the evaluation of INSET are encouraged to come together regularly, e.g. two to three times per year, to inform each other of promising developments and to discuss other relevant issues.

3. Some of the more promising work that has, or is currently being, undertaken, such as the studies mentioned in this report, should be made more widely known, perhaps through Evaluation Newsletter or the British Journal of In-Service Education.

In conclusion, I would like to express my appreciation and thanks to all those who have supplied me with information, and to apologize if some of them feel that I have done their work less than justice.

Chapter Three

A NATIONAL PERSPECTIVE*

Ray Bolam, University of Bristol

Introduction

The national enthusiasm for the in-service education and training (INSET) of teachers which was legitimated and stimulated by the James Report has been followed by a considerable growth of interest in the evaluation of INSET. However, it seems clear from several studies (McCabe, 1978; Taylor, 1977; Borich, 1978) that, although a great deal of practical work is going on, considerable disagreements about some fundamental conceptual and methodological issues remain. This paper, therefore, has two main aims:

(a) to review relevant literature and experience;

(b) to highlight some of the main issues and implications for national INSET policy.

A national perspective makes it essential that the evaluation process be considered at various levels. Accordingly, an analytic or conceptual framework devised for a comparative study of INSET in ten OECD countries (Bolam, 1978) is used as the organizing basis for the literature review. This framework (Figure 1) distinguishes between three major factors in the evaluation process - the evaluator, the evaluation target and the evaluation tasks. These three factors are conceptualized as open social systems but particular account is taken of the way in which their members - individuals and groups - perceive and affect these social systems throughout the evaluation process. Thus, the framework's underlying theoretical stance is that the systems and action frames of reference can be treated as complementary (cf. Greenfield, 1975).

*This is a revised version of a paper originally given in January 1978 at a national conference on INSET policy, sponsored by the Department of Education and Science and the Advisory Committee on the Supply and Training of Teachers, at Bournemouth. I am grateful to those conference participants and colleagues in the Bristol School of Education who commented on the draft paper; it was printed in the British Journal of Teacher Education in January 1979, 5, 1.

The framework assumes that there are important evaluation tasks at each level - teacher, school, agency, local and national - and adopts a very broad concept of evaluation, embracing what might usually be regarded as research and survey data collection. Its basic proposition is that an understanding of an INSET evaluation process depends upon a careful analysis of the characteristics of the evaluation task, target and agent and, more specifically, upon the way in which these three factors interact in any one cell of the model.

The Targets of INSET Evaluation

An obvious first question is: What exactly is being evaluated? Dimension 3 of Figure 1 indicates that the main evaluation targets are likely to be INSET policies and programmes at all levels. The term policy is used here to embrace the rationale, aims and structure of an overall INSET policy; for example, a school's staff development policy or a teachers' centre's overall policy on course and activity provision. The term 'programme' is used here to cover the components of that policy in action: for example, a particular course run by a college of education or a curriculum development workshop run by an LEA adviser.

A subsidiary question might well be: What is the purpose of the evaluation? In the field of curriculum evaluation, Scriven (1967) distinguished between formative evaluation, which occurs during the course of a programme and is used to modify it, and summative evaluation, which occurs at the end of a programme. In practice, this distinction is rarely clear-cut (Stake, 1976), not least because programmes frequently contain subprogrammes and may be used for several cohorts. For example, the evaluation of the 1974/5 stage of the pilot induction scheme in Liverpool was summative for that year but formative in relation to the overall, four-year scheme.

Thus, an evaluation may be centred on a policy or a programme, at one or more levels, and may be formative or summative. We can be more precise if we ask the further question: What is the focus of the evaluation? Stufflebeam et al. (1971) distinguish between four focuses - context, input, process and product. Here, too, the types overlap but the typology is useful in clarifying the main thrust of an evaluation.

Context evaluation compares intended with actual system performance, analysing the context and questioning existing and alternative system goals. Several INSET evaluations of this broad type have been carried out at national level: Taylor and Dale (1971) surveyed the characteristics and induction training needs of probationers; Townsend (1970) surveyed the in-service needs of teachers. In recent years there have been several major reviews of policy on teacher education, including INSET: there was the 1969/70 Parliamentary Select Committee on teacher education, the Area Training Organization (ATO) reviews, which were produced as separate reports by each university ATO, and the James Committee (James Report, 1972). The Induction and In-service Training Sub committee (INIST) of the Advisory Committee on the Supply and Training of Teachers (ACSTT) has published several discussion papers reviewing INSET needs and questioning widely held assumptions about the goals of INSET. These various reviews led first to the White Paper (Great Britain, DES, 1972) and eventually to a new Green Paper (Great Britain, Parliament, 1977c) both of which may be regarded as arising from national 'evaluations' of policy. Similar context evaluations of local authority INSET policy have been made (e.g. Cane, 1969; Canter, 1978); and no doubt many more have been conducted but not published.

The aim of input evaluation is to 'provide information for determining how to utilize resources to meet programme goals' and several examples of this focus are identifiable in the UK: Hammond (1975) reviewed the contribution of ATO/DES courses; the second INIST discussion paper reviewed available resources; Her Majesty's Inspectorate reviewed the contribution to INSET of certain colleges (Great Britain, 1977a); the contribution to INSET of LEA advisers has been studied by Bolam et al. (Great Britain, DES, 1976); Bradley (1978) has reviewed national INSET financial and resource issues; Henderson et al. (1975) produced a very thorough review of provision in the Oxford ATO. No national evaluation has, as yet, tried to quantify comprehensively the 'input' of the various INSET agencies and there is no doubt that some feel undervalued. For example, twenty-six professional subject associations recently formed a Council of Subject Teacher Associations to try to ensure that their views were heard at national level (Doe, 1976).

Process evaluation concentrates on monitoring the actual process of programme implementation, asking such questions as: Who does what to whom, when, where and how? Process evaluation has been a major feature of the third year of the Teacher Induction Pilot Schemes Project (Baker, 1977). Three process-style evaluations associated with curriculum projects are also worthy of note since both projects had a substantial emphasis on INSET. Elliott (1977a) has raised important issues associated with the evaluation of the dissemination process of the Schools Council Progress in Learning Science Project. Arnold et al. (1977) have issued a brief interim report on the impact of the Avon Resources for Learning Development Unit's classroom demonstrations, which are a novel form of INSET, on teachers and departments. The Ford T Project had a similarly direct orientation towards classroom practice and concentrated on a process evaluation (Elliott and Adelman, 1973).

Product evaluations concentrate on programme effects, frequently using behavioural objectives. Taylor's (1977) survey contains several references to INSET evaluations which have concentrated on products or outcomes. Henderson (1978) gives a salutary account of the complexities of evaluating the outcomes of an Open University post experience course on reading, and demonstrates that valid conclusions about the long-term effects of a course must be based on data from interviews and observation rather than simply from questionnaires. Perrott (1977) studied the effects of self-instructional micro-teaching courses on the teaching performance and attitudes of experienced teachers immediately and then four months after the course itself. Bolam (1973) evaluated in-service courses for probationers in four authorities in terms of their effects on general professional attitudes and self-perceived knowledge, judgement and behaviour. Bradley and Eggleston (1977) evaluated a variety of unsponsored induction schemes in the East Midlands using attitude scales and diaries. Advisers in Suffolk LEA have devised a multi-faceted scheme which appears both comprehensive and practical and is described in Chapter Three of Part Two.

The INSET Evaluation Task

A second major question might be: What does the task of evaluation consist of? The funded researcher has to negotiate an evaluation contract with his funding or sponsoring body and then to negotiate entry and continuing access to the target (e.g. a school staff) of the evaluation. The internal evaluator may not at first sight appear to have to do these things and certainly may not identify them as explicit and separate tasks. But if he is, say, a professional tutor who has been asked by his head to evaluate a staff conference, he will need to establish and clarify his terms of reference, the resources (e.g. time) available to him and the purpose of the evaluation, i.e. he has to negotiate the terms of his 'contract'. He will then have to obtain the agreement of colleagues to be questionnaired, interviewed or observed, i.e. he has to negotiate entry. He will need to implement his design, however simple, and analyse his data. Subsequently, he may also have to negotiate with his colleagues about the way in which the findings are interpreted and disseminated, particularly with the head. All six sub tasks identified in Figure 1 have to be carried out; the method of doing so will vary, as we shall see, according to the status of the evaluator and the nature of the overall task.

Any actual evaluation design is dependent upon negotation between the evaluator, the sponsor and the people in the evaluation 'target group'. It is important to be clear, moreover, that action research evaluation designs are not immutable. In practice, they are redefined and renegotiated as a result of experience, policy changes and other contextual events, and the differing perceptions and behaviour of the people involved. Even within an evaluation team, significantly different notions of the evaluation task may co-exist and these, too, will change over time. It is for these reasons that the model underlying Figure 1 conceptualizes the 'evaluation task' as a social system.

Several factors are likely to influence the acceptability and ultimate success of any particular evaluation. These factors are invariably subjective and are thus likely to be judged differently by the various people involved. One of the first sets of questions to be asked about a design concerns its relevance to the task in hand, its feasibility in terms of implementation and its competitive strength as against other evaluation designs. The answers to this set of questions might well turn upon the magnitude and scale of the proposed evaluation (e.g. would the pupils have to be questionnaired as well as classroom teachers); upon the degree of evaluation involved (e.g. interviews about personal as well as professional life); upon the divisibility of the evaluation (e.g. would all teachers in an LEA have to be questionnaired or just a sample); upon the complexity and communicability of the design; upon its compatability with the values of the members of the sponsoring body and the target group (e.g. 'your criteria are inappropriate for what we are trying to do'); and upon its adaptability (e.g. 'can the heads be dropped from the interview sample?').

Finally, we come to some fundamentally important factors associated with the costs and benefits of an evaluation. These benefits and costs may be actual or perceived, material or non-material and initial or continuing. Material costs may relate to finance (e.g. 'this is simply too expensive'); output (e.g. 'the results won't be worth it'); time (e.g. 'we are too busy to fill in all these questionnaires'). Non-material costs or benefits may relate to administrative or decision-making arrangements (e.g. 'all these meetings will be too disruptive' or 'highly beneficial'); to personal or professional status or prestige (e.g. 'I stand to lose face if the evaluation is unfavourable' or 'Being associated with this project adds to my prestige and opens up promotion possibilities'); and to aims not envisaged by the evaluators (e.g. 'this observation schedule would make a good teacher assessment form'). In general, we can agree with House (1972) that those on the receiving end of an evaluation (e.g. the person running an INSET course) have little to gain and a lot to lose from an evaluation. We should not be surprised if they avoid it or adopt strategies to reduce the threats it poses, for instance by co-opting an evaluator into the action programme and hence into their value system. Conversely, action projects which offer personal and institutional benefits are likely to find it easier to have evaluation accepted as a necessary but tolerable price.

The INSET Evaluator

A third broad question concerns the characteristics of evaluators and evaluation teams. The evaluator may operate at any one of the five levels in Figure 1 and may be internal or external. Thus, an individual teacher could decide to evaluate personally the effectiveness or an INSET course in which he had participated by completing a self-rating scale or assessing his pupils' performance in the light of the changed methods adopted as a result of the course. Alternatively, he might seek the assistance of a school colleague (e.g. a professional tutor) or an outsider (e.g. the course organizer) to do this. Usually, of course, the teacher will be content to make a much more informal, unsystematic and private appraisal.

At school level, the members of staff will similarly vary in the extent to which they formally research an INSET activity. In preparation for an INSET day conference, staff from one comprehensive school devised, administered to themselves and analysed a questionnaire on language across the curriculum. The DES-funded project on Schools and In-service Teacher Education (SITE), on the other hand, involves an external evaluation team using an extensive range of evaluation approaches and instruments (Baker, 1977).

At the external providing agency level most courses probably go unevaluated, but Taylor (1977) summarizes some interesting evaluations carried out by staff in colleges while Davis, in Chapter Four, Part Two, gives a sensitive account of the difficulties faced by teachers' centre staff in evaluating their courses.

At LEA level, the job of monitoring and evaluating the effectiveness of overall INSET provision has rested with the advisory staff, but the evidence available (Bolam et al., 1976) suggests that advisory teams have concentrated on making this provision rather than on formally evaluating it.

At national level a similar pattern can be discerned. HMI have actively promoted a great deal of INSET but have published few evaluative accounts of individual courses or of overall national provision. Such accounts have generally been the work of funded projects or ad hoc committees.

A major recent development has been the introduction at all levels of posts and machinery for INSET decision making and evaluation: for example, professional tutors or their equivalent and staff development committees in schools; INSET co-ordinators and course development units in colleges (Collier et al., 1977); LEA advisers with specific duties for co-ordinating INSET and LEA consultative/advisory committees on INSET: and, at national level, the INIST Subcommittee. These individuals and groups may evaluate INSET within their own settings although they usually lack the resources to adopt sophisticated methods.

The increasing use of evaluators who are external, funded, professional researchers is another relatively recent and important development. The rest of this section concentrates on such evaluators to highlight some key issues; but these issues will be no less real and relevant for many internal evaluators.

The evaluator's status, authority, power and basic values, his formal relationship with the funding or sponsoring body and with the members of the target group, are all of fundamental importance in influencing the methods and outcomes of an evaluation. MacDonald (1976a) distinguished between three 'political' evaluation styles. The bureaucratic evaluator gives an unconditional service to the funding or sponsoring body, accepting its values and giving it control over his data and his recommendatory report. The autocratic evaluator gives a conditional service to the funding body, deriving his values from his academic peers and retaining control over both the data and his recommendatory report. The democratic evaluator gives his service to the community at large, regardless of who is funding him; recognizes value pluralism; gives his informants control over data; and makes no recommendations - in a report which he writes in a popular style. These are, of course, 'ideal types' and MacDonald does not suggest that they will necessarily occur in their pure form in the real world.

In a similar vein, Elliott (1977b) distinguished between two ideal-typical extremes, evaluation from above and from below. He argues that a bureaucratic understanding of INSET, in which it is viewed 'as a form of social-engineering for rectifying a defective system' will tend to lead to evaluation from above, i.e. from the standpoint of the sponsoring educational administrator. On the other hand, a professional understanding of INSET, in which teachers' experience of the INSET process is regarded as of greater importance than any intended outcomes or product, will tend to lead to evaluation from below, i.e. from the standpoint of the participating teacher.

It is for these and related reasons that professional evaluators have paid increasing attention to the nature of the contract which they enter into with the sponsoring or funding body (Stake, 1976). One of the most basic choices facing any evaluator is the political or ideological position from which he is prepared to negotiate a contract.

The next strategic choice facing the evaluator concerns his approach to methodology. INSET evaluation is essentially a form of action or evaluation research. Hemphill (1969) argued that, unlike classical experimental research, in evaluation research the selection and definition of the evaluation problem or task is not under the control of the evaluator; precise hypotheses cannot usually be generated or tested; the study can seldom be replicated; data collection is dependent upon both feasibility and the actions of other people; variables can rarely be controlled either by randomization or by the use of control groups.

The assimilation of these and related ideas to curriculum evaluation in the UK has been summarized admirably in several recent studies (Tawney, 1976; Hamilton, 1976; Hamilton et al., 1977). The central issue has been the appropriateness of experimental designs, as classically expounded by Campbell and Stanley (1963) for evaluation research in education and there is no doubt that professional opinion has shifted considerably. The arguments for this shift were most effectively deployed by Parlett and Hamilton (1976), who distinguished between designs in the agricultural botany tradition and those in the anthropological tradition which they called illuminative evaluation. Illuminative designs are now much more commonly used by professional researchers than hitherto, though the debate about their usefulness is still very much alive.

A third critical, and fundamental, choice facing the evaluator concerns the criteria to be used for determining the effectiveness of the INSET policy or programme. However desirable it may be to establish the impact of INSET on pupil behaviour or achievement, this is unlikely to be technically possible in most situations. What, then, of the effects of INSET on teacher behaviour and performance.

It is a reasonable enough expectation that INSET should have some impact on teacher behaviour, but the difficulties of establishing the nature and extent of that impact must not be underestimated, whether it be in the symbolic, simulated or real modes (Turner, 1973). Many studies have included evaluation of teacher behaviour in the symbolic mode using questionnaires and interviews (e.g. Bolam, 1973; Bradley and Eggleston, 1977; Hoste, 1978; Henderson, 1978); only one assessed simulated teacher performance in a laboratory setting (Perrott, 1977); several did so in real classroom settings, but usually using instruments which were informal, as in Suffolk, or of the self-report type (Henderson, 1978). The case for systematic observation in real settings is well argued by McIntyre and MacLeod (1977).

Another difficulty concerns the use of instruments and research designs based on behavioural objectives. This debate has gone on in the curriculum evaluation field for a generation and has now been extended to include teacher education. The behaviourist position is well known: curriculum designers should specify their aims in terms of behavioural objectives so that their effectiveness can be judged in terms of observable behavioural outcomes. This approach underpins performance or competency-based teacher education programmes, as exemplified in Cooper et al. (1973) and Turner (1973). Critics of this approach reject the assumption that teaching can be meaningfully analysed into detailed behavioural objectives, argue that the sum of such behaviours does not adequately represent good teaching and point to the way in which the approach has become bound up with the accountability movement in the USA (Smith, 1975)'. However, as Stones (1973) points out, none of this is to deny the potential value of clearly specifying objectives in teacher education.

The critics usually advocate alternative methods - for example the case study and portrayal - of describing behaviour in educational settings (Hamilton et al., 1977). There is some disagreement amongst advocates of 'alternative' evaluation about the extent to which the personal characteristics of the target group members should be included in the final 'portrayal' (MacDonald, 1976b).

There would probably be no disagreement amongst evaluators about the desirability of including a consideration of financial costs in the evaluation. The problem is the general unavailability of the information. Procedures for costing INSET vary considerably around the country and reliable information is scattered and scanty (Bradley, 1978). Thus, it is frequently simply not possible to give other than a crude, global estimate of INSET costs. Financial costs, like teacher performance, are extremely difficult to evaluate, and educational administrators and politicians are likely to be disappointed in seeking hard, clear evidence of success or failure in cost-effectiveness terms.

In summary, any would-be evaluator is faced by a number of important decisions: about his political relationship with the sponsoring body, and the target group; about research design, criteria and methodology; about control of access to data; about personalization of data; about adopting a descriptive or judgemental role; and about the style and form of the dissemination. This brief account has presented the options in ideal-typical and even dichotomous terms, but this is, of course, an oversimplification. It may be true that the responses of evaluators have tended to cluster into something like MacDonald's three, or even Elliott's two, types but it is far from clear that this is unavoidable. Illuminative designs may have overemphasized process evaluation, but some shift in emphasis was necessary and Parlett and Hamilton (1976) are certainly clear that multi-faceted designs are desirable.

One of the most encouraging recent developments in the USA has been the use of research methodologies which employ a variety of quantitative and qualitative techniques, and evaluation teams which include people with a wide range of skills. Schwartz et al. (1977) report on an INSET evaluation study which adopted a social systems model as its theoretical framework and a transectional evaluation model which included six types of data collection and analysis; quantitative and psychometric; ethnographic; historical; managerial; comparative case study; and classroom learning environment. Fox (1977) describes six previous evaluations of the massive Teacher Corps programme. He argues that they use a predominantly standard, rather than illuminative approach to evaluation and concludes that they had little value for policy decision making or understanding. He himself has directed a multi-disciplinary evaluation team which used a variety of techniques (Fox, 1976) and has argued the need for exploring the utility of quantitative methodologies within a broadly illuminative approach (Fox and Hernandez-Nieto, 1977).

Approaches of this degree of complexity and sophistication have not yet been used in INSET evaluations in the UK but recent experience indicates that they could be. Thus, Perrott (1977) has demonstrated that a classical experimental design is appropriate for certain purposes in INSET evaluation. The various approaches to evaluation in the sponsored and unsponsored pilot induction schemes (Great Britain, DES, 1977b; Bradley and Eggleston, 1977) point to the need to develop multiple methodologies. Developing experience and theory in related fields is also of considerable relevance: Jenkins (1976) has described a useful typology of methods in curriculum evaluation; Burgoyne and Stuart (1977) distinguished between the manifest characteristics of programmes (e.g. content, length, location) and their core processes or implicit learning theories; and concluded from a study of 14 management development programmes that their effectiveness is related to these learning theories; finally, innovation theory can tell us a great deal about barriers to the successful implementation of INSET courses and the changes which they are designed to promote and about the essentially dynamic and interactive nature of the innovation (and evaluation) process over time (e.g. Bolam, 1978; Hoyle, 1976; MacDonald and Walker, 1976; Fullan and Pomfret, 1977).

Some Implications for National Policy

INSET evaluation can be, and is being, carried out by a whole range of practitioners - teachers, professional tutors (or their equivalents), lecturers, INSET co-ordinators, advisers, HMI, professional associations and INSET committees at school, college, local authority and national levels. Given the likely growth of INSET in the medium and long term and the need to evaluate INSET now and in the future, it is abundantly clear that it would take an army of outside researchers to do the job; it is equally clear that this would be a totally impractical solution.

Although finance and logistics dictate that self-monitoring and self-evaluation of INSET are likely to predominate, we should also recognize that these are, in any case, desirable activities for a profession. If effective self-evaluation is to be carried out then three main steps must be taken. First, the appropriateness of the formal self-evaluation agents and procedures (e.g. the appointment of professional tutors, LEA co-ordinators and the setting up of units and committees) should be reviewed at each system level - school, providing agency, LEA and national. Second, relatively simple and easy-to-use self-evaluation procedures should be developed: these will need to build upon existing practice in schools, colleges and LEAs and to be further refined by drawing upon the methods of professional researchers (e.g. Steadman, 1976, for a helpful review). Third, key people like professional tutors and INSET co-ordinators in colleges and LEAs should be given the opportunity to attend short practical evaluation training courses.

Many of the problems and issues outlined in this paper will only be serious ones for the professional researcher working on contracts to evaluate INSET programmes and policies. Funding bodies need to be aware of these problems, too, and need to recognize their implication for the research contract and the subsequent implementation of the research design. Researchers need to consider carefully the implications of adopting and advocating one particular style of evaluation: specifically they should beware of an exclusive adoption of process evaluations and equating these, simplistically, with illuminative evaluation. Recent experience both in the USA and in the UK suggests strongly that a pluralistic evaluation strategy, in which a variety of disciplines and techniques - both qualitative and quantitative - are employed, may well be feasible and more productive - both practically and theoretically.

Two main prerequisites are necessary if pluralistic strategies are to be adopted. First, researchers must be equipped through their training and experience to decide what approach is appropriate for a particular task. Second, national funding bodies and research agencies must be prepared both to use larger, multi-disciplinary research teams for appropriate tasks and to look to the career and training needs of researchers. In addition, professional researchers should acknowledge an obligation to contribute to the development of the evaluation guidelines for INSET providers suggested above.

Quite understandably, the principal and fundamental concern of those who have to provide the resources for INSET is: are we getting value for money? LEA administrators and advisers, for example, need to be able to convince their local politicians that it is worth spending money on INSET at the expense of, say, smaller classes or another local authority activity like housing or the social services. Ideally, they would like 'hard' information about the effects of a particular INSET programme on teacher performance, or, even better, on pupil performance. One aim of this paper has been to demonstrate the complexity of this request. Normally such product measures will be unattainable but sometimes they will be attainable, at least in a semi-hard form or for a part of a programme. One purpose of the three-dimensional framework is to facilitate the formulation of more specific and answerable requests for product evaluation and to distinguish these from those aspects which are more amenable to, say, process evaluation. To do this, each cell of the model has to be considered separately in relation to any particular evaluation task.

The need for certain kinds of context evaluation at all levels is evident. Initially, there is a need to clarify the definition of INSET - for example, does it include MEds and PhDs as well as short courses? Does it include preparation for new roles, e.g. headship, or, as in some European countries, only training of a role maintenance kind? There is also a need for more appropriate strategies and procedures for the regular collection of the following sorts of contextual information: teacher needs; system needs; available resources; activities and programmes; evaluation procedures; costs; research and development activities; consultation and planning procedures. Another task for context evaluation would be to seek to explore the relationship between INSET and continuing or recurrent education for adults (Lynch, 1977).

Equally evident is the need to carry out input evaluations on the changing roles of particular agencies. For example, what is happening to teachers' centres and teacher centre wardens as a result of the financial crisis, the move towards accountability and the increasing involvement in INSET of advisers? Or, what are the policy implications of the various kinds of INSET Advisory Committees which are being set up around the country?

Finally, policy makers and funding bodies have a responsibility for funding studies of ways of improving INSET evaluation. Several of the suggestions in this section ought to be considered in this light.

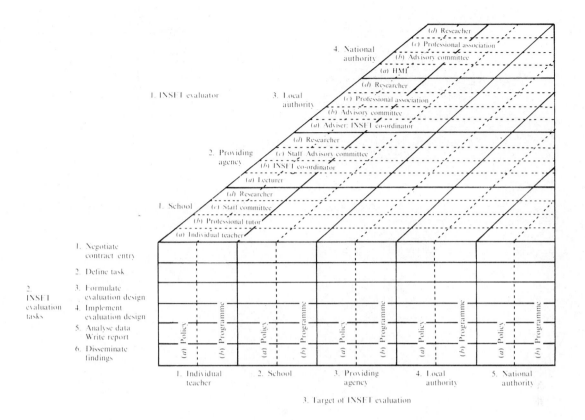

Figure 1: Inset evaluation: an analytic framework.

PART TWO
SOME CASE STUDIES

INTRODUCTION AND EXPLANATION OF THE CHOICE OF CASE STUDIES

This part is designed to explore by means of case studies the need for viable models and strategies for the evaluation of INSET. It complements Bolam's (1976) case study which defined areas of INSET provision and particularly outlined the evaluation procedures being used in the Teacher Induction Pilot Schemes (TIPS) Project. As Bolam illustrated, a wide range of agencies is found to be providing extended teacher education in the United Kingdom, among them being:

- Local education authorities;
- The Schools Council;
- The area training organizations and their successors, often in association with the Department of Education and Science (which also provides courses of its own);
- The BBC;
- The Open University;
- Universities, polytechnics and institutes of higher education.

To give a reasonable picture of the state of the art this paper draws its examples from as many of these as possible.

Introduction

The evaluation of in-service work for teachers can be thought of as being in three 'orders' or ranks. The first, or most elementary, order is that which involves only simple, but carefully thought out 'feedback' techniques. The sort of investigation which can be built into an in-service course or programme. Jordanhill College, in Glasgow, as has been mentioned, has taken such techniques a long way but most of the agencies are provided with and sensitive to 'first order' evaluation. Cornwall LEA, with its follow-up letters at the end of the year to all course members; Northumberland LEA, with a developed three-part report on each block-release course for new teachers; Sunderland Polytechnic, with a range of course evaluations; Dundee College of Education, which has its report forms completed by each member of a course, and after last afternoon discussions arranges visits to them in their schools and reporting back sessions - these are just four examples of widespread good 'first order' practice.

The 'second order' is a stage beyond this, when evaluation becomes a more professional activity, and when evaluators become conscious of themselves. Techniques, approaches, reactions and principles are studied and defined, discussed and discriminated between. Evaluation becomes much more than natural sensitivity, feedback and responses to questionnaires. Independently appointed evaluators are often called for and their net is cast wider than individual course conclusions. This is the 'order' which the best probing, progressive practice seems to have reached in the United Kingdom in the INSET field. The influence of ideas of democratic (Macdonald et al., 1974) and illuminative (Parlett and Hamilton, 1972) evaluation are still being worked out. It is with techniques of this order that this paper is concerned.

A transition from first to second order can perhaps be identified at the stage where wider studies of in-service needs and opinions have been carried out. Gloucestershire (Garnham et al., 1973), Nottingham (Bradley, 1975), Manchester (Taylor, 1973) and especially the survey carried out over the whole of Scotland (National Committee, 1975), are examples of such studies. The last named gave teachers 'an opportunity to express their views about in-service training' and sought to 'obtain a more precise quantification of current and future provision', besides obtaining an assessment of how teachers use what they learn on in-service courses. National planning of INSET in Scotland can thus go forward from a firm base.

The third order is attained not just by the evaluation of wider schemes but also by the reporting of the reception of such evaluations and the whole organizational response to them. This order, of which examples occur among Stake's case studies (Stake et al., 1976) has probably not yet been represented in the United Kingdom INSET work, but the induction pilot study approaches this level.

It is, however, at the level of the second order that resistance to evaluation can be recognized, where doubts and a sense of being threatened can arise, and tendencies to avoid or disregard the work of evaluators become apparent among some teachers and administrators. The way past such barriers seems to lie in the more general appreciation of what evaluation is about, in more open discussion and in a wider spreading of knowledge about techniques; in short, in more in-service education about evaluation.

Explanation

The case studies selected for this paper, besides including examples which illustrate work with as many of the 'providing agencies' as possible, are meant to reflect the present situation and needs in the United Kingdom. They therefore try to:

1. show what sort of evaluation is being practised;

2. give clear explanations of techniques and their results;

3. indicate how evaluation has been applied in each of the
   'agencies' areas;

4. bring out some of the doubts and difficulties encountered.

The first studies supply three examples of the evaluation of courses
designed to teach reading, although they illustrate quite different
approaches and contexts for evaluation. They are: Hoste (Stirling)
describing an opinion seeking approach to the evaluation of a one-
term course; Henderson (Open University) reporting (i) a multi-faceted
approach to the evaluation of an Open University course, (ii) a small
scale questionnaire approach to the evaluation of nine short courses.

These are followed by: Elliott (Cambridge Institute) on the evaluation
of the dissemination stage of a curriculum innovation; this example
involves a discussion of the principles and problems underlying the
use of a 'democratic approach', a review of an LEA (Suffolk) approach
to the INSET teaching of evaluation techniques; Davis (Liverpool) on
the evaluation of the work of teachers' centres and school-based
INSET springing from the induction project; Baker (Bristol) on national
evaluation co-ordination.

The range of the case studies therefore extends from the clear-cut to
the more complex and tentative, from local to national, from straightforward course evaluation through to John Davis's acute and immediate
account of the problems met in evaluating the work of a teachers'
centre and in introducing school-focused INSET. This account brings
an intelligent and critical but friendly regard to bear on this possibly most important of developments.

New work being done in promoting and evaluating school-based programmes,
based on Bristol University, will yield considerably more information
and produce guidelines appropriate to this area. An interim evaluation
by Keast and Carr (1979) indicates that evaluation will be based upon
reports by consultants who would in turn obtain 'feedback' from participating teachers. It is interesting that they refer to the role of
consultant as being akin to that of the psychotherapist guiding a
patient towards a solution to his problems.

Chapter Four

THREE EVALUATION STUDIES OF COURSES FOR TEACHERS OF READING

(a)   The evaluation of a one-term college course
Roland Hoste, University of Stirling

This study deals with the methods adopted for producing information about a one-term in-service course for teachers of reading. The course was based on the Open University postexperience course PE 261, and the evaluation was carried out for the National Foundation for Educational Research. It was intended that the information produced would be used by tutors, together with other data gathered intuitively, in deciding what modifications might be advisable in future versions of the course.

The view held throughout the Colleges Curriculum Project[1] was that tutors are ultimately responsible for judgements upon their courses. The NFER role in the Project was to devise ways in which information about courses can be made available to tutors. The Project took a deliberately eclectic view of evidence, accepting that both verbal and numerical symbols are valid representations of reality. Zelditch (1962) notes that:

> There is, in fact, a tendency to be either for or against quantification, as if it were an either/or issue. To some extent the battle lines correlate with a relative concern for 'hardness' versus 'depth and reality' of data. Quantitative data are often thought of as 'hard', and qualitative as 'real and deep'; thus if you prefer 'hard' data, you are for quantification and if you prefer 'real and deep' data you are for qualitative participant observation. What to do if you prefer data that are real, deep and hard is not immediately apparent.

This did not seem to present a problem to the Project. It seemed clear that these two types of data are really complementary and that in order to obtain the fullest understanding of the impact of a course all available data should be considered.

We agreed with the comment by Stockhausen (1973) who, writing of biography, stated: 'Like the mosaic of a notorious criminal casebook: nothing is irrelevant, anything can become a clue.' In the Project's view, the same can be said of evaluation.

The approach may be clarified by taking an example from another sphere. For five centuries King Arthur's Round Table has decorated the wall of the Great Hall of Winchester. Recently, the table had to be removed during the renovation of the building, thus providing an opportunity to date it. Several sources of evidence were sought: an expert in medieval joinery examined the structure; a dendrochronologist studied the growth rings of the timber used in the construction; radio-carbon dating was employed; radiography was used to determine whether the painting on the surface covered any earlier decoration; an art expert gave an opinion on the date of the visible painting. The evidence (reported in _The Times_, 21 December, 1976) from the joinery expert established that the structure was indeed a table - mortices to take the tenons on the legs were present. The table appeared to have been made between 1250 and 1350 to judge from the method of construction. The dendrochronology experts found that the pattern of growth rings in the timber pointed to the trees having been felled in 1335, or alternatively (but less convincingly) in 1228. Radio-carbon dating pointed to a date of felling of 1330 plus or minus 60 years.

However, the painting on the surface was found not to cover any other decoration, and the style of the draperies suggested that the painting was the work of artists about 1510.

Later, a letter to _The Times_, 4 January, 1977, drew attention to the Issue Rolls of the Exchequer which, in 1356, show a payment of £26.13.4d for 52 oak trees from woods near Reading for the construction of 'The Round Table' at Windsor. A subsequent letter (15 January, 1977) suggested that 'The Round Table' referred to was in fact the building erected by Edward III to house the Feast of the Round Table in 1344. Perhaps the Round Table now at Winchester (which would never have required 52 oak trees) had been intended for the Round Table building in Windsor as an embellishment to Edward's romantic cult of the Arthurian legend. (It also showed how long Edward III took to settle his debts!).

Thus evidence assembled from a number of mutually independent sources all points to the same conclusion: that the construction on the wall at Winchester is a table, and was most likely made between 1335 and 1345.

None of the evidence is clear-cut (an alternative date might fit the growth ring pattern; the radio-carbon dating has a wide margin of error; the joinery style gives only an approximate date; and the historical evidence is hedged with a number of speculations) but taken together the weight of the evidence is impressive.

In evaluation, the evidence available is often similar in nature - capable of alternative explanation, surrounded by margins of error, approximate, and hedged with speculation. But the more mutually independent sources which can be tapped to provide information, the more likely it is that we shall be able to come to some fairly positive conclusions about our courses.

The Reading Course presented a number of problems for gathering evaluation data. Firstly, the numbers on the courses were small, effectively eliminating statistical approach. Secondly, the college was 65 miles away from the Project base, inhibiting any intensive participant observation.

The techniques adopted involved a blend of observation, interview, discussion, semantic differential rating scales for each unit of the course, and a post-course questionnaire. These methods will be briefly described, together with a sample of the type of data which results.

Observation and Discussion

The Project officer sat in on a number of sessions throughout the course, keeping notes of the main trends, especially any which seemed to him to raise particular problems for tutors or students. Many of these points were raised later in interview with both groups of participants.

Group discussions were used on a number of occasions to discover the opinions of staff and students. These discussions have some advantages over face-to-face interviews in that the discussants are represented en masse and perhaps are not overawed by an evaluator as they might be in a one-to-one situation. Conversely, if there are disagreements within the group, individuals tend to keep their opinions to themselves in order not to offend their colleagues. These discussions can stray away from the point and so need to be tactfully controlled by 'seeding' - introducing new topics about which information is being sought, and so steering it back to productive lines of development.

An example of the information that can be obtained about a course arises from such a 'seeded' discussion between a group of seven of the teachers on the course and the members of staff who had taught it. The Project's research officer was primarily an observer who took little part in the discussion, but when he did it was a normal part of the proceedings, arising out of the interchange of ideas among the participants. Two local authority advisers also took part.

The aim of the discussion reported below was to discover what effect the course had had on teachers' reading styles and teaching techniques in the six months following the course. It took place as part of a workshop in which teachers could exchange ideas and experiences which might be helpful to one another. The discussion was seeded mainly by members of staff, but the teachers also sparked each other into fruitful exchanges. The discussion was tape-recorded by the Project research officer.

The developments raised seemed to fall into eleven interrelated areas, which were dealt with in turn in the draft report to the tutors on which the following commentary is based. Only one of these areas is discussed in detail here.

The effect on students' activities in school

It is clear that the course had stimulated a number of developments in the schools of those who attended the meeting. Some of the changes mentioned are:

> In one school the reading books had not been looked at critically since the teacher joined the school five years previously. Since returning from the course each book had been appraised individually. The teacher has now compiled a list of books suitable for reading to classes in the school. In another school the teacher had remained after school until 9.00 PM on several occasions in order to read and classify the books.

Another member of the course now discussed with children exactly what purpose they had in mind in reading and what they expected to obtain from the particular book they were reading.

The next teacher claimed he now ignored the 'blurb' on the inside front cover; he tended to 'skim' a book rather than read it from cover to cover to discover if he wanted to use it with his class. Previously, he had not had the time to read in advance the books he used and therefore many had been unsuitable although he had often not discovered this until they were read by the children.

Many teachers felt the course had made them aware of the concept of readability and they now used it in selecting books. The Fog Index described in the course was found to be cumbersome and there was a general feeling that a book's level of required reading ability could be appraised by scanning it, noting the big words it contained and the size of the print, etc.

Some eight other main changes could be similarly identified in this area alone.

The other ten areas which were recognized in discussion and about which information was obtained were:

New activities which did not arise directly from the course, but resulted from attending it.

Facilitators and inhibitors of changes in the school.

Changes in teaching method.

Appraisal of previous teaching style.

Effect on teachers' own reading.

Comments on the course materials.

Attitudes teachers held before the course.

Reactions to the course.

Organization of in-service training.

The data provided by group discussions

This almost totally unobtrusive data-collecting technique has provided us with a considerable amount of information about this course, which will enable its tutors to make some judgements about it. No doubt they would formulate some opinions from their participation in the discussions, but perpetuating the proceedings by tape-recording then enabled the evidence to be sifted at leisure, and a more permanent document for future intakes' reactions to the course or perhaps with those of teachers attending other in-service courses.

The semantic differential scales

The scales were produced and validated in a variety of contexts in teacher education earlier in the Project's life. Profiles of two of the course units are illustrated in Figures 1 and 2. These two units provide an interesting contrast. Unit 2, Literature for Children, shows a profile which can be seen to be more extreme than the mean scores on most scales for all units. (These mean scores are shown by crosses in the diagrams.) It was therefore seen as more useful, good, enjoyable, etc. than most.

In contrast, Unit 7, Developing your own Reading, is seen as less extreme on most scales. Thus while it is still rated 'relevant', it is seen as less relevant than the average unit.

The indications here are that elements of the course with direct practical application in the classroom were rated more favourably than those elements concerned with enhancing a teacher's personal expertise.

In conclusion

It must be apparent that the course members thought highly of their experience. The mean scores on the semantic differential scales (crosses in Figures 1 and 2) show that course members rated the course overall as useful, good, enjoyable, coherent, satisfying, clear, valuable, relevant, informative, interesting and stimulating. The discussions show that they were clearly stimulated to innovate when they returned to the schools. The post-course meeting of ex-students provided opportunities to extend their influence to other course members. The discussion 'rambled' and was often seemingly irrelevant to course evaluation, but many of the rambles raised points of value in planning future courses. For example, much of the discussion dealt with the problems of teachers returning to their schools. The reactions from colleagues were often not what had been expected. Instead of a welcome they were received with apathy, even hostility and resentment. Clearly, innovation cannot take place in this climate and this, therefore, raises questions about course structure. Should the course spend time on strategies teachers might adopt for implementing new materials and methods in a disinterested atmosphere? Should the course be totally restructured and go, as suggested, to the schools as a sort of travelling circus?

FIGURE 1: *Semantic differential profile for* Unit 2: Literature for Children

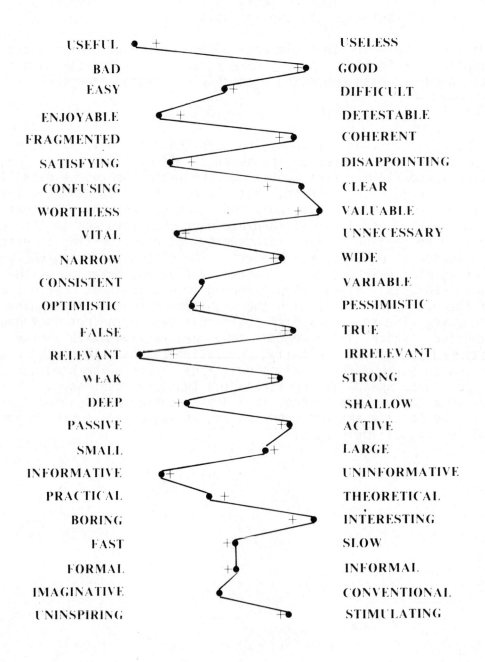

FIGURE 2: *Semantic differential profile for* Unit 7: Developing your own reading

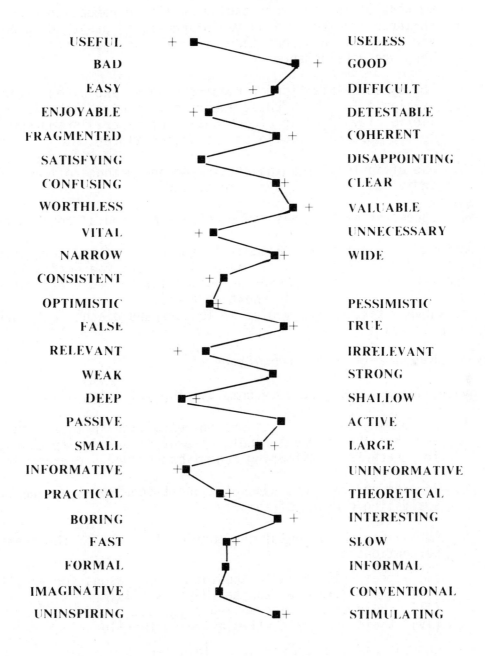

(b)   The Evaluation of an Open University Course
Euan S. Henderson, the Open University

Between October and December 1972, nine short courses under the title
<u>The Teaching of Reading: Basic Techniques</u> were organized by an area
training organization at different centres throughout its region. A
total of 317 teachers enrolled in the nine courses. Each course consisted of three, four or five evening sessions, totalling about six
hours. The course tutors were briefed to cover the following content:

1. methods of introducing reading skills to reception class
    children, including a survey of published pre-reading books
    and materials and home-made materials and games to aid
    language development;

2. survey and evaluation of reading schemes and wider literature
    available for the 5 to 12 age range, with an emphasis on
    flexibility in using a combination of materials appropriate
    to the particular child or group of children;

3. use of tests of reading attainment and methods of recording
    individual children's progress: and

4. causes of backwardness in reading and remedial approaches.

The content briefing did not attempt to impose on course tutors the amount
of time to be devoted to each of these topics, and the emphasis varied
from one tutor to another. Nevertheless, all tutors did attempt to cover
all four areas. In courses as short as these, the intention was no more
than to survey, through the medium of lecture and discussion, current thinking and practice.

Aims and Methodology of the Evaluation

The evaluation was designed to accomplish the following aims.

1. To examine teachers' reasons for enrolling in these courses
    and thus the appropriateness of providing the same course
    for teachers of differing school background and experience.

2. To examine the usefulness of a questionnaire as a means of
    evaluating courses of this type.

3. To analyse the value of the courses in terms of the teachers'
    perceptions of

    (i)   their relevance to the teachers' reasons for enrolling;
    (ii)   their effect on the teachers' skills;
    (iii) their effect in changing classroom practice; and
    (iv)   their effect in stimulating further learning;

    and to examine whether any of this series of nine similar
    courses produced significantly 'better' or 'worse' results
    than the others in these terms.

4. To test the hypotheses that practical outcomes of in-service training are more probable when (a) several teachers from the same school undergo a similar training experience and (b) when systematic arrangements are made for teachers who have been involved in the in-service training experience to feed back their perceptions of this experience to other members of the staffs of their schools.

It was decided to accomplish these aims by devising a simple questionnaire, administered a sufficiently long period after the end of the courses to provide the opportunity for some of the possible outcomes to be apparent. A draft questionnaire was prepared and piloted on a group of teachers who had attended another reading course of a generally similar type to those being studied. A copy of the final questionnaire was sent to each of the 317 teachers six months after the courses had finished. The questionnaire was accompanied by a letter, explaining that it formed part of an investigation to discover the effectiveness of the courses, assuring confidentiality, and requesting completion and return of the questionnaire within one month.

The response rate was 29 per cent. No attempt was made to follow up those who did not reply to the first request. This return rate was disappointingly low, but four checks were available to judge how representative this sample was of the total enrolment: the distributions of respondents and non-respondents between courses, between employing local education authorities, between types of school, and between rates of maintenance of attendance. The distributions were not significant between the nine courses, between the four local education authorities represented, and between the four types of school represented. The distribution of respondents and non-respondents in relation to maintenance of attendance was, however, significant ($p < .001$), the response being greater from those who had attended every session.

Thus in terms of distribution between courses, employing authority and type of school, the response to the questionnaire appeared to be representative of the total course membership. This gave some confidence that, in spite of the low overall return, conclusions drawn by analysis of the 90 responses would have some validity. In terms of the level of attendance, on the other hand, the response was significantly greater from those who maintained fuller attendance. As one reason, at least, for falling off in attendance might well have been a degree of dissatisfaction with the course, there was an implication here that caution would need to be exercised in extrapolating to the course membership as a whole any conclusions about the degree of satisfaction expressed by respondents.

Teachers' Reasons for Enrolling

On one item in the questionnaire, course members were asked to 'indicate, as specifically and briefly as possible, your reasons for enrolling in this course'. The range of responses was very wide, from the vague to the highly specific. Content analysis of the responses indicated that they could usefully be classified into seven categories, as shown in Table 1.

Over 40 per cent of respondents gave reasons which fell into more than one category. On the other hand, over a quarter of respondents (27 per cent) gave no specific reason for enrolling. (This includes those who gave entirely unspecific reasons and those who indicated only a desire for meeting and talking with colleagues.) Also, many of those whose reasons fell into one of the specific categories were not very precise in indicating what they hoped to gain from the courses. This raises questions about the extent to which teachers diagnose their needs and relate such diagnosis to a decision to enrol in an in-service course.

Correlations were sought between the categories of need expressed and various personal and experimental characteristics of the teachers involved (e.g. length of teaching experience, type of school) but no significant relationships were found. This finding contrasts with that of Smith et al. (1970) who concluded that: 'Elementary teachers of different grades and with different terms of service express different attitudes, needs and preferences regarding their training to teach reading'; but it is more in line with a replication of Smith's study by Rutherford and Weaver (1974), who concluded that: 'Teaching level and years of experience do influence training preferences, but...variances within grade and experience levels may be greater than variances between levels.'

Assessment of the Utility of the Questionnaire

Four items on the questionnaire were designed to obtain four measures of the value of the course to the participating teacher.

Table 1: Reasons for Enrolling in the course

	Number of responses	Responses as % of respondents
1. To find out about new reading schemes and/or books	43	48
2. Opportunity of discussion with colleagues	29	33
3. To learn techniques for teaching slow learners and/or diagnosis of reading difficulties	19	21
4. To find out about new apparatus and/or games	14	16
5. To find out about the teaching of pre-reading skills and/or diagnosis of reading readiness	11	12
6. Other specific reasons	4	5
7. Unspecific reasons	17	19

MEASURE 1: 'How relevant did you find this course in relation to your reason for enrolling in it?' A three-point scale was provided: 'very relevant', 'fairly relevant' and 'irrelevant'. Teachers responding 'very relevant' were distinguished from those using the other two categories.

MEASURE 2:   'In your own opinion, has attending this course increased your skill as a teacher of reading?' This question was open-ended: teachers responding with an unqualified affirmative were distinguished from those offering qualified or negative responses.

MEASURE 3:   'Have you, or have colleagues at your school, implemented any ideas arising from the course? If so, please indicate as specifically as possible what these ideas were.' This measure, at least assuming truthfulness, might be said to be somewhat less subjective than measures 1 and 2. Teachers giving some form of positive response were distinguished from those giving negative responses.

MEASURE 4:   'Have there been any other ways, not mentioned above, in which you or your colleagues have followed up your attendance at this course?' This measure, like measure 3, falls into a subjective/objective category. Those reporting some form of follow-up activity were distinguished from those reporting none.

The intercorrelations between these four measures were examined by calculating the phi-coefficients and examining their levels of significance. The intercorrelations of measure 4 with the other three measures were all positive, but in no case reached a significance level of $p = .05$. It is perhaps not surprising that stimulation of further learning was not a reliable measure of the value of courses which were, after all, designed as self-contained learning units, and in which this was not a declared objective. It was, however, an important side-effect. All the intercorrelations between measures 1, 2 and 3, however, were highly significant ($p < .001$). Thus teachers who perceived the courses as very relevant in relation to their reasons for enrolling were likely to consider that their teaching skills had improved as a result of attendance at the courses and to report implementation of ideas from the courses in their schools. It may be that respondents did not perceive the three questions as distinct and that an element of response set is responsible for these intercorrelations. In view of the very different nature of the questions, however, this does not seem very likely. A possible explanation is that the relevance of the courses to certain teachers' needs enabled them to utilize ideas in their schools and led them to believe that they were teaching reading more effectively after the courses.

Analysis of the Value of the Courses

1.   On measure 1, 41 per cent of respondents described the course they attended as 'very relevant', 48 per cent as 'fairly relevant' and 11 per cent as 'irrelevant'. There were no significant relationships between teachers' views of the relevance of the courses and the length of their teaching experience or the type of school in which they were working. Nor was there a significant relationship between the perceived relevance of the courses and the reasons(s) teachers had given for enrolling. For example, a high proportion of course members (33 per cent) had included a desire for meeting and talking with colleagues from other schools amongst their reasons for enrolling and, although no special provision for this kind of interchange was made in the courses, approximately half of the teachers including this reason for enrolling said they found the courses 'very relevant', and half had found them 'fairly relevant'.

65

2.   On measure 2, 34 per cent of respondents said the course had increased their skills as teachers of reading, 16 per cent indicated a slight improvement with responses such as 'a little', 'to a certain extent' and 'slightly', and 38 per cent replied 'no'. The remaining 12 per cent of respondents indicated that the course had given them more confidence in their existing skills. One third of respondents giving an unqualified positive response to this item was not a high proportion, especially since, as mentioned above, it might be expected that, taking non-respondents into account, the proportion of the total membership of all the courses doing so would be even smaller. Once again there were no significant relationships between a positive response to this item and teachers' length of experience, type of school or reasons given for enrolling.

3.   On measure 3, 31 per cent of respondents indicated that no ideas had been implemented. The 69 per cent of respondents who indicated that they had implemented some ideas provided a wide variety of responses. Content analysis of these suggested seven categories (with some response including more than one category), distributed as shown in Table 1. There were some clear correspondences between these categories of school outcomes and the categories of reasons teachers gave for enrolling shown in Table 2. Enrolment reasons 1, 3 and 5 correspond clearly to outcome categories 1, 3 and 5, and enrolment reason 4 to outcome categories 4 and 6. Of the respondents who replied to both the relevant items on the questionnaire, 23 per cent reported implementing ideas in the same category as their reasons for enrolling. On the other hand, 28 per cent of those who replied to both items reported implementing ideas in categories which did not correspond to their reasons for enrolling. Furthermore, the category of outcomes which included the third largest number of respondents ('Introduction of new methods of presenting work') was not related to any of the reasons given for enrolling in the courses. This again raises questions concerning the matching of teachers' needs to their decisions to enrol in a course. It may also be, however, that attendance at the courses in itself assisted teachers to diagnose new needs.

4.   Measure 4 was intended to discover whether any follow-up learning had been undertaken as a result of attendance at one of the courses. 30 per cent of respondents did not reply to this item, and of those who did 75 per cent indicated that there had been no such follow-up. The remaining 16 teachers described a variety of means by which they had attempted to learn more about the teaching of reading. Two described a visit to a local centre for the teaching of reading (one a personal visit and one by several members of staff, not all of whom had attended one of the courses). Two, both from the same school, described a visit by most of the staff of their school to their course tutor's school. Two, both from the same school, said that it had been as a result of attendance at one of these courses that four months later they had attended a more substantial vacation course on the teaching of reading. Three teachers, from two schools, had arranged for the tutor of the course they attended to visit their schools and talk in one case to staff and in the other case to staff and parents. One teacher indicated that she had found the reading list provided by her course tutor 'invaluable to me for private study'. The remaining six teachers, from five schools, described visits made to other schools which they said had been inspired by attendance at the courses. In one case the visits had been undertaken by an individual; in the other cases several staff from each school had been involved, not all of whom had attended one of the courses.

66

Table 2: Ideas Implemented from the Course

		Number of responses	Responses as % of respondents
1.	Trial and/or purchase of new reading schemes or books	20	24
2.	Introduction of new methods of presenting work	15	18
3.	Introduction of new diagnostic and/or remedial approaches for slower readers	6	7
4.	Introduction of new language development and reading games	17	21
5.	Introduction of new pre-reading ideas and material	9	11
6.	Introduction of new apparatus	5	6
7.	Other ideas implemented	7	8
8.	No ideas implemented	26	31

The evidence that certain of the nine courses had been, in various senses, more satisfactory than others was striking. Teachers on two of the courses perceived them as significantly more relevant (p = .0056), reported significantly more frequently that their teaching skills had been improved (p < .001), and reported significantly more school outcomes (p < .001) than teachers who had attended one of the other courses. Of these two courses, one was perceived as 'better' than the other on all three measures. This much greater level of success of two of the nine courses did not appear to be attributable to differences in the composition of their course memberships, since no course differed significantly from the others in terms of the experience of the teachers involved or the types of school in which they were working. These results indicate the utility of this method of evaluation for making comparisons between courses, since in spite of the absence of absolute measures of the value of the courses (particularly in view of the low response rate on the questionnaire), relative measures were obtained. These are useful, as here, in studying a series of similar courses held concurrently, and would also be useful to examine changes in the effectiveness of a course which is repeated in successive years.

Feedback from the Courses to the Schools

Twenty per cent of respondents reported no feedback from the courses to other staff in their schools. Of those who indicated that there had been some feedback, there were wide differences in its extent and thoroughness, but it was possible to distinguish approximately equal numbers of teachers for whom feedback had been a casual process (41 per cent) and for whom it had been a more systematic and structured process (39 per cent). Systematic feedback was not reported significantly more or less often from any particular type of school, and there was no relationship between the extent of feedback and teachers' perceptions of the relevance of the courses. Feedback was, however, reported significantly more frequently by those teachers who considered that the courses had had a substantial effect on their teaching skills ($p < .05$). Systematic feedback was also significantly more frequently reported from those schools which also reported practical classroom outcomes of the courses ($p < .02$). In general, therefore, there appeared to be a link between the extent of feedback and perceptions of the courses' value in terms of both personal and school outcomes.

Further examination of the data indicated another factor which influenced both feedback and the extent of school outcomes. Of the schools whose teachers had returned questionnaires, 36 per cent were represented on the courses by more than one member of staff. Systematic feedback was significantly more frequently reported from those schools from which more than one member of staff had attended ($p < .01$). On the other hand, only slightly more schools reporting outcomes were those which had been represented by more than one member of staff and this was not significant. A possible interpretation is that attendance of several members of staff at the same or similar courses was likely to lead to more feedback, which in turn was likely to lead to more outcomes.

Interviews conducted with five headteachers who had attended one or other of the courses themselves, together with one or more colleagues, provided some support for this causal sequence. All five supported the view that beneficial effects had stemmed from more than one member of their staffs attending courses at the same time. Three of the five also acknowledged the importance of structured feedback, and two of these expressly supported the view that attendance of several members of staff had led to useful feedback, which in turn had led to ideas from the courses being implemented in the schools. It was from these two of the five whose headteachers were interviewed that the most noteworthy school outcomes had been reported on the questionnaire.

68

(c)   *The Evaluation of Short Courses using a Questionnaire*
   Euan S. Henderson, the Open University

[3]The Open University course <u>Reading Development</u> was first presented in 1973:

> This course is intended to help students to understand all levels and all aspects of the reading process and how to guide the development of reading competence throughout the school years. Opportunities will also be provided for the student to appraise and improve his own level of reading proficiency.
>
> Throughout the course students will be provided with a variety of activities integrating theory with practice.
>
> Although this course will concentrate on the child in the middle years of school, consideration will also be given to:
>
> (a) the early stages of reading;
> (b) special problems;
> (c) advanced reading.
>
> In the latter part of the course students will be given the opportunity to concentrate their studies on a particular area. (Open University, 1972)

The course was presented in four successive years, up to 1976. In all four years it was offered as a 'post-experience' course to a total of 4,409 teachers who enrolled only for this particular course. In its latter three years it was also offered to the University's undergraduate population, 5,105 of whom took the course as a contributory half-credit to the 6-credit BA degree (and 82 per cent of whom were practising teachers). In 1977 this course was replaced by a new version, under the same title.

Most Open University courses are evaluated after presentation, at greater or lesser depth, using routine and/or <u>ad hoc</u> procedures. The main aims of such evaluations are threefold:

1. to obtain baseline data to aid the University's decision making in relation to all its courses, for example to compare workload between courses (Blacklock, 1976);

2. to provide early warning of any serious problems encountered by students during the first year of presentation, in the hope that they can be corrected, or at least alleviated by 'stop press' announcements to the first year group, or at worst, by making amendments to the course before the second year of presentation; and

3. to provide data which can be utilized when the time comes for remaking or replacing the course (usually after between four and eight years of presentation), some of which may be course-specific and some of which may provide more generalizable insights into the processes of teaching and learning at a distance.

Several evaluation procedures were applied to Reading Development, each focusing to a greater or lesser extent on one or more of these purposes. They can be conveniently classified into two types: process evaluations, which sought to obtain information on the success or otherwise of the course as a learning experience, and product evaluations, which set out to discover the impact of the course on teachers' school practices. The first type of evaluation is common to most Open University undergraduate courses; the latter is peculiar to those courses, like Reading Development, which have direct vocational implications.

Process Evaluations

Most Open University courses, during their first year of presentation to the undergraduate population, are surveyed in two ways, *via* the tutors (Bates, 1974; Moore, 1978). Both procedures were used in 1974 for Reading Development.

Davey (1975) invited all the post-experience students (586), together with a systematic random sample[4] of 485 (about one fifth) of the undergraduate students to complete a series of report forms for single or double units[5] of the course immediately after studying them. The questionnaires sought opinions on workload, difficulty and interest of each unit, usefulness of the broadcast components, contacts with tutors, etc., all in the form of pre-coded items, as well as providing space for open-ended comment on various aspects of the material. The response rate, typically for this procedure, ranged from about 35 per cent on the earlier units to about 10 per cent on the later ones.

Moore (1974) invited all 102 course tutors to complete a series of report forms, one for each unit of the course, at four points during the year. The questionnaire asked tutors if any of the printed materials or broadcasts required alteration and, where appropriate, invited suggestions for improvement. Tutors were also asked about their experiences in marking assignments and in conducting class tutorials. The response rate, again, typically, ranged from 25-45 per cent.

The findings of the two studies were broadly similar. The response rates for these procedures are not good, but it is not their intention to seek absolute measures of worth of the various teaching media used on a course, but rather to provide comparative data. Thus Unit Text 7 of Reading Development (Augstein and Thomas, 1973) was rated as 'very' or 'fairly' interesting by only 39 per cent of respondents, as against 79-97 per cent for every other unit (Figure 1), and was also rated 'very difficult' by a much greater proportion than any other unit text (Figure 2). The fact that this unit text was also one of the two which most tutors thought needed alteration (Figure 3) confirmed that there was cause for concern here. Similarly, the first of the twelve television programmes fared worst on every measure. The data were not always so clear-cut, however. For example, Unit 1, which most tutors considered was in need of alteration (Figure 3), was one which was rated 'very' or 'fairly' interesting by a high proportion of students (Figure 1) and found 'very difficult' by relatively few (Figure 2).

Figure 1: *Students' Ratings of Interest of Unit Texts*

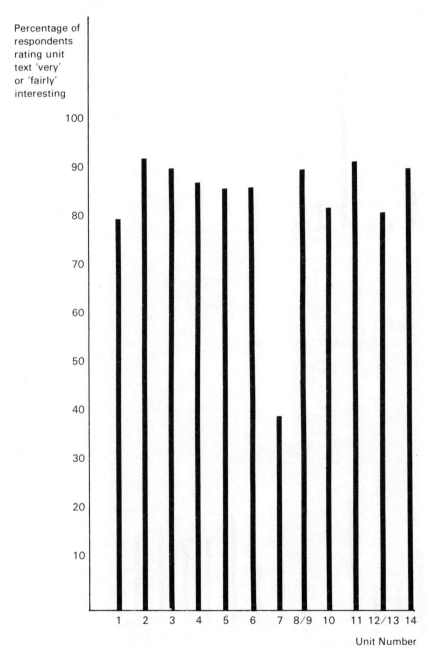

Percentage of
respondents
rating unit
text 'very'
or 'fairly'
interesting

Unit Number

Figure 2: *Students' Ratings of Difficulty of Unit Texts*

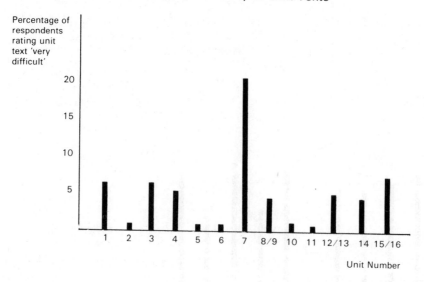

Figure 3: *Tutors Recommending Alteration of Unit Texts*

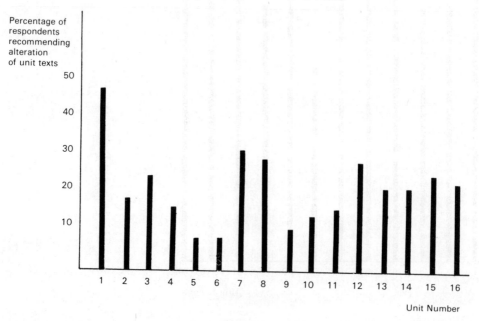

This kind of information contributes to all three aims of Open University course evaluation. The routine nature of these procedures is important in providing baseline data to enable at least crude comparisons to be made between courses. On some courses it has given early warning of crises. Although no severe problems occurred on Reading Development, the first television programme, for example, was remade for the third year[6] of the course. Also, some of the data was of value to the course team which undertook the preparation of the completely revised version of the course for presentation in 1977.

Product Evaluations

Some six months after the first cohort of 1,321 post-experience students had completed the course, McHugh (1974) sent each one a specially designed questionnaire. Apart from sections devoted to collecting personal and occupational details about respondents, the main section of this questionnaire listed 21 techniques and ideas discussed in Reading Development indexed to the relevant sections of the course, and asked teachers to which areas of their work they had been, were being, or would be applied - for example to their own reading or to their work with children. Respondents were asked to indicate whether they had been using these techniques/ideas before they started the course, while they were studying the course, and/or since the end of the course. The response rate was 38 per cent.

The overall impression from teachers' responses to this questionnaire was of a rather low usage of the techniques and ideas before the course, with a substantial increase during the period of the course, which was maintained, or fell away only marginally, during the following six months. Averaged over all of McHugh's 21 points, the pattern was 16 per cent users before, 39 per cent during and 37 per cent after. This, however, masks a number of important differences in the usage of individual techniques and ideas, which can be illustrated by three typical examples.

1. Some techniques were already being used by teachers fairly extensively before the course and the increase in usage was marginal. For example, 39 per cent of respondents said they were having children write stories for use with other children (Moyle, 1973) before the course; this increased to 45 per cent during the course and to 47 per cent in the subsequent period.

2. Some techniques which were little used before the course were taken up by a rather large proportion of teachers. Thus only 11 per cent of respondents were assessing individual children with the aid of an informal reading inventory (Hunter and Merritt, 1973) before the course, but 46 per cent said they were doing so during the course and 41 per cent afterwards.

3. Other techniques which had been little used before the course had a much lower take-up rate. For example, 6 per cent of respondents were using various methods of recording reading strategies (Augstein and Thomas 1973) before the course, compared with 17 per cent during, and 14 per cent in the following six month period.

73

However, in spite of such variations in the extent of application, the general finding of this study was that there had been substantial take-up of the various techniques and ideas from the course in classrooms during the period that teachers were studying it and little, if any, 'method-reversion' (Williams, 1966) afterwards. But this finding was based on teachers' reports of their own activities, and required checking by a more objective method. A small number of students who responded to the questionnaire were therefore followed up with interviews in their own schools in two separate studies.

In one of these, 21 teachers were interviewed to investigate how far Reading Development concepts and procedures had been applied during the year after they completed the course. The researcher concluded:

> There is large-scale enthusiasm for the course; students have been genuinely stimulated. The comprehensive concept of reading seems to have given students valuable new insights. Some students have been able to pursue their new-found deeper awareness in a practical way in the classroom but there are many...who can offer little solid evidence of (Reading Development) approaches in the classroom...So far there is evidence of only a fairly limited follow-up of reading skills...There is a lot of evidence that information about the course is being disseminated by students. The material has been discussed on courses and in staff rooms although it is not clear at all how far this has led to any positive action...Overall there is a striking contrast between the situation indicated by the students on (McHugh's) questionnaire and the actual situation in the classroom now. It looks as if students tried out materials and approaches for the (assignments) or the Unit activities but failed to integrate them into their general teaching programme. (Ellis, 1975).

In the other study ten teachers were interviewed, selected from those who had said that they were using, both before and after studying the course, two of the techniques/ideas listed in McHugh's questionnaire, concerned with the development of resources for reading and the organization of resource units (Moyle, 1973). They were asked to describe their present work in the classroom, with particular reference to such resources. The research concluded:

> The earlier affirmative answers to resource work, in (McHugh's) questionnaire, tended to evaporate under scrutiny. A particular feature of resource work may be present in the school but very rarely were there several features...Any major use of a retrieval system was not in evidence...There was little idea of a total review of the work undertaken by teachers. Instead description of work concentrated on small-scale innovations or recent activities rather than on illustration of a continuous overhauled progress...Assessing the difficulty of innovation depended on whether any innovations could be seen to threaten the school structure outside the classroom or be thwarted by the structure within the classroom. For instance, in several schools isolation of the teachers from each other in the classroom was encouraged by the conservative nature of the school and Head. Shortage of money and an indifferent or hostile Head were mentioned. Above

all, time was a constant factor in rejection of practical work from (Reading Development)...In general, an ad hoc rather than systematic approach to (Reading Development) depended on the practicality of the specific example. Rejection depended mainly on whether the component was felt to be universalistic, complicated or demanding of time and in particular, whether the attitude expressed in 'outside schools looking in' was present. Regarding the work on resources as complete innovation, failure was (the) predominant result. Attitude toward reading and its resources was changed, but not practice. The organization of the school and the experience of the teacher were main factors in adoption of innovation. (Lawn, 1974)

These studies focused largely towards the 1977 remake of the course. It was evident that Reading Development had been of great interest to the many teachers who had studied it, but that the enthusiasm it had generated had failed to lead a substantial proportion of these teachers to utilize the techniques and ideas discussed in more than a fragmentary way in their classrooms. In revising the course, therefore, the course team attempted to emphasize a more systematic approach to reading development. The evaluation also implied that the new course should enable teachers to develop new skills in the context of their working situations. In the words of the prospectus for the 1977 version of the course:

The course is essentially a series of workshops...The primary aim... is to provide students with a wide range of practical experience in helping children or adults to develop their reading. This will involve being able to organise learning activities to ensure progressive development of the range of reading and reading-related skills that are necessary to meet the demands of adult life. Theoretical studies are only introduced, therefore, when they bear directly on some immediate teaching problem. In addition, the necessary theoretical insights are developed by means of exploratory work by the student...(who) carried out a brief diagnostic study of children or adults, and goes on to select or design appropriate teaching materials or strategies. These are immediately tried out on the children/adults, and the results are then evaluated so that methods and materials can be modified in the light of experience. (Open University, 1976)

Notes

[1] A joint project conducted by the University of Leeds School of Education and the National Foundation for Educational Research: The Project was sponsored by the Department of Education and Science. Open University course PE261 was in this case used as the basis for one term's intensive study. Henderson's later paper describes a multi-faceted evaluation of the course in its intended OU one-year pattern.

[2] The two following articles by Euan Henderson are given in the amended form in which they appear in his book The Evaluation of In-service Teacher Training (1978). . I am grateful for permission to use them thus.

[3]The author is indebted to Peter Davey, Jim Ellis, Martin Lawn, Roy McHugh and John Moore for making available evaluative data collected by them; to Studies in Education Ltd. for permission to reprint this modified version of Henderson (1977). The original version of this Exhibit was presented at the 1977 Annual Conference of the Society for Research into Higher Education 'Student Learning now: what, how and why?' and was published by the Society in 1978 as part of the conference proceedings. Other evaluations of the course described in this Exhibit have been published by Cooper and Sellors (1977) and Hoste (1977).

[4]Discussion of sampling procedures has been omitted from the present volume, since the numbers involved in in-service training activities are usually small enough to warrant sending a questionnaire to all participants. Excellent discussions of the technicalities of sampling are available elsewhere (e.g. Moser and Kalton, 1971).

[5]The term 'unit' is used to describe one week's work (average 10-14 hours) on a full-credit Open University course, or a fortnight's work on a half-credit course. The core of each unit is usually a specially written correspondence text, which may be associated with a variety of other components - radio, television, readings from set books, assignments, supplementary materials of various kinds, tutorials etc. A full-credit course normally has 32 units and a half-credit 16.

[6]A 'course team' at the Open University is comprised of a number of subject matter experts and other specialists (television and radio producers, educational technologists, editors, graphic designers, etc.). All aspects of course production are the team's collective responsibility (Riley, 1976).

Chapter Five

THE EVALUATION OF THE DISSEMINATION STAGE OF A SCHOOLS COUNCIL PROJECT

John Elliott, Cambridge Institute of Education

Introduction

A conceptual scheme which maps relationships between research/evaluation activities and in-service education constitutes a methodology to guide the researcher's practices. Methodologies need not be explicit. Frequently they remain as taken-for-granted assumptions embedded in the practice of research/evaluation. It is only when established procedures are felt to be in some sense problematic or when there are no established procedures in a particular area of inquiry that methodological self-reflection becomes a preoccupation of the researcher/evaluator. In-service education is a relatively new field of inquiry but inasmuch as it is a form of education one might feel that traditional methodologies of educational research would be appropriate if it were not for the fact that they have been very much called into question in the last decade.

This paper is the product of a process of reflection about my own conduct of a piece of evaluation research in the field of in-service education which ended in August 1977. The process began with an attempt to design the study prior to the research, and has continued throughout it. It has not simply involved thinking about the problems of method in the light of a conceptual scheme generated prior to the study, but also clarifying and modifying the scheme itself in the light of the problems encountered along the way. This is why I have chosen to write a methodological paper in the form of a case study. I wanted to show that methodology is not something which is appropriately cooked up in the 'armchair' by theoreticians and then applied by researchers and evaluators, but something which develops from continuous reflection about the practical problems encountered during the conduct of a particular study.

The In-service Programme

I was appointed on a part-time basis from January 1976 to August 1977 to evaluate the dissemination of the Schools Council's 'Progress in Learning Science' (PLS) project to teachers in five local authorities in England.

---

*An adapted version of a paper given to a conference in June 1977 and subsequently published in the British Journal of In-Service Education, Winter 1977.

The appointment was made by Wynne Harlen, the Project director, in consultation with the Schools Council and the grant-holder for the Project. I was given freedom to design my own evaluation study on the understanding that this limited study would generate insights into the problems and possibilities of dissemination through in-service courses and meetings and feed future decisions with respect to the dissemination of both the PLS project in particular and other projects more generally.

The trial dissemination plan conformed very much to Schon's 'proliferation of centres' model. The idea was for the central team to disseminate the project to LEA representatives at two conferences in the Summer of 1976; and for the five local authorities to be free to make their own decisions with respect to patterns of dissemination at the local level.

Four of the five LEAs involved opted for a school-based pattern of in-service work. The fifth opted for meetings at a teachers' centre drawing on teachers from different schools.

Three LEAs opted for school-based in-service work under the leadership of heads and/or senior staff. Only one opted for a school-based pattern led by members of the advisory service.

Of the three 'school-based led by heads' areas the heads in one did not attend the LEA representatives conferences. Their access to the Project was mediated by a teachers' centre warden.

The somewhat diverse patterns which emerged gave an opportunity to study how they influenced teachers' perceptions and reactions to the programme.

The Emergent Methodology

The methodology of research/evaluation into in-service teacher education which has emerged from this dissemination study can be specified in terms of the following conceptual framework.

Dimensions of Research/Evaluation	Related Concepts	Key Justificatory Concepts
Access to research reports	Democratic	The public interest
Aims	Formative	Programme development
Content	Critical theory	Autonomy through self-monitoring
Perspective	The 'underdogs' advocate	Justice
Process	Dialogue	Respect for persons

The left-hand column refers to different dimensions along which relationships between research/evaluation and in-service education might be conceptualized. The centre column specifies the relational concepts themselves. The right-hand column specified what I have called 'Key Justificatory Concepts' because they provide a rationale against which the methodological concepts listed in the middle column can be justified. The reader may at this point wonder what the connection is between the justificatory concepts and the object of the research/evaluation enterprise; namely, in-service education. I hope to make this clear by the end of the study. In the meantime I will simply claim that the 'key justificatory concepts' specify criteria for assessing a worthwhile process of in-service teacher education. In other words the ideal process is one:

1. which protects and fosters the public interest;

2. which is open to on-going development;

3. where in-service personnel have control over their own actions (autonomy);

4. where in-service personnel treat the views and practices of the teachers involved justly and with respect.

The methodological concepts listed in the middle column are embedded in a context of social and educational values which together characterize the ideal form of the process under scrutiny. This explains something the reader may already have detected; namely, my difficulty in separating research from evaluation as discreet activities. The separation assumes the validity of distinctions between facts and values, theory and practice. Implicit in the conceptual framework I have outlined is a rejection of these assumptions. One cannot in the study of social activities like in-service teacher education avoid the fact that methodology is embedded in an evaluative position which structures one's observations and hypotheses.

Methodology in Action

Dialogue

In the five month period leading up to the conferences for LEA representatives one of the first things I did was a literature search on innovation processes. From the search I noted hypotheses which were either explicit or implicit in the work of various writers. The exercise also helped me to reflect about some of the hypotheses which were tacit, but not consciously formulated in my own thinking, about dissemination in in-service contexts. In the end this dialogue with the literature resulted in a list of hypotheses being circulated to the Project Director and LEA representatives either prior to, or during, the Summer 1976 conference.

The point of this exercise was to inform the in-service personnel whose activities I was studying of the 'theories' which would guide my observations and interview questions; at least in the initial stages of the study. Possessing this information they would then hopefully be able to assess the extent to which I was selecting, interpreting and explaining data to fit my 'theories' rather than allowing the data to test them.

The communication of hypotheses to those being studied was a dialogue procedure for checking bias in the researchers' selection and analysis of data. From the beginning of the study I had quite consciously conceptualized the relationship between myself and the in-service personnel involved in the dissemination as one of dialogue. I had used the communication of hypotheses procedure in the initial stages of research before, but in the context of the study of teaching on the Ford Teaching Project.

The reader might well ask why it was necessary to adopt a dialogue procedure for checking against bias. I felt reasonably clear about this at the time. Many of the hypotheses we generate to explain the conduct of people in social situations make either explicit or tacit reference to their intentions and motives. The researcher has access to these mental attributes indirectly through the observation of indicative behaviour. But the agents of the conduct themselves have direct and privileged access through introspection. There is a sense in which they are in the best position to know their own states of mind. This does not mean that they are infallible. People can be unconscious of, and therefore mistaken, in their accounts of their intentions and motives. But human beings possess the capacity to reflect about their unconscious states of mind and thereby to become self-aware. It is this capacity which enables them to become self-determining persons with some control over their future conduct.

To ignore a subject's capacity for self-reflection, and being unwilling to enter into dialogue with him, constitutes disrespect for persons. There is an intimate connection between respect for persons and objectivity in social research, the former being part of the latter. Disrespect for an individual's capacity for self-reflection constitutes an unwillingness to entertain disconfirming evidence; a failure on objectivity.

The hypotheses list I produced was primarily useful in stimulating dialogue with the project director, Wynne Harlen, who led the conferences for LEA representatives, and there were occasions when, knowing my 'theories', she was able to point out what she felt to be cases of bias.

The concept of dialogue also heavily influenced the way reports were written, circulated and released. Up to the present time I have completed three major case studies. The first focused on the negotiations between Wynne and LEA representatives about the in-service organization of dissemination within the five trial areas (see 'From Project to LEAs Part 1' Interim Working Paper VI (Elliott, 1977))*. The second was about the two LEA representatives' conferences (see 'From Project to LEAs Part 2' Interim Working Paper VII (Elliott, 1977))*. The third consisted of a study of Schools Council decision making and influence with respect to the development of the Project and its materials prior to the dissemination trials. A fourth covered the dissemination of the Project within the trial areas.

The writing of the reports went through three main stages:

1. My interpretation and analysis of data collected by observation (in the case of Working Papers VI and VII) and interview (in the case of the Schools Council Study).

    I attempted to separate my analysis from the data on which it was based. Analysis - interpretation and explanation - was presented in a different type to that used to write verbatim accounts of observed verbal exchanges or interview data. This hopefully enabled the reader to assess the relationships between evidence and assertion.

*These may be consulted on application to the Schools Council Research Team.

2. The report was then circulated to participants referred to in my study and they were asked to respond to my analysis, both in the light of their own accounts of the reported events and the data contained in the report itself. They were also given opportunities to suggest clarifications, elaborations and even exchanges. (In the case of Working Paper VI and VII the reports were circulated first to the Project Director for comments and suggestions, and then a second draft, incorporating these, was sent to LEA representatives).

3. On receiving replies I amended the purely descriptive sections in the light of participants' suggestions. I then cut up their responses to my analysis, and juxtaposed them opposite the specific comments they referred to. General comments on the report as a whole were placed at the end. At first I intended to include all responses at the end but one discerning member of the PLS consultative committee pointed out that this would be a good way of guaranteeing that no one would read them. She then suggested the juxtaposition procedure, for which I am extremely grateful to her.

4. A second draft, documenting the dialogue with the evaluator, was circulated to the participants, asking them whether they agreed to its general release. The primary audience were disseminators working either in the trial programme or concurrently outside the trial areas.

Two of these 'dialogues' are now accessible to disseminators and researchers. The third, on Schools Council decision making with respect to the Project, was in second draft and being discussed within the Council. The fourth report on the dissemination within LEAs was about to enter stage 2*. The time span between the completion of stage I and release had varied from 3 to 6 months.

The dialogue reports involved subjects as active partners in research, in the same way as the Ford Project (which I directed) involved teachers and pupils in classroom research. In my view, dialogue is a key methodological concept in any form of educational, or more generally social, research. Dialogue is a condition of respecting one's subjects as persons and as such indicates an objective attitude towards their conduct.

Criticism, Justice and the 'Teacher's Advocate'

While reflecting about my entry hypotheses in the early weeks of the study I realized that the majority tended to place the conduct of developers and disseminators in a more critical light than that of the teachers on the receiving end. Moreover, the hypotheses tended to specify and explain constraints on teachers' critical access to ideas of the planners and leaders of in-service provision.

*The third report, 'Thinking Aloud' (Elliott, 1977), may be consulted by researchers on application to the Schools Council Research Team. The fourth appears as part III of the project's final report, 'Portrait of a Project' (Schools Council, 1980).

I began to see the study as committed to the view that teachers ought to have the freedom to express their criticisms of the content being disseminated and that their views should receive just treatment. It is this commitment to freedom and justice which justifies conceptualizing the researcher as the teacher's advocate in in-service contexts.

But I began to realize about half-way through the study that the value-position I had clarified had general methodological implications for social inquiry. It required me to take the teacher's perspective in in-service contexts because in such contexts the teacher is 'the underdog', and justice is basically concerned with the rights and freedoms of those in subordinate positions within the social hierarchy. Inasmuch as in-service teacher education involves hierarchical relationships between people of different status with respect to the content of the communication, justice requires the researcher to study such activities from the perspective of the teacher.

My first three major case studies were not focussed on relations between in-service personnel and classroom teachers. The second of these was a study of a researcher (the Project Director) disseminating her Project to a group consisting largely of LEA advisers and headteachers. Reacting to my report, some LEA representatives indicated that they didn't like the Project Director being the critical focus, and felt that questions about their opportunities for critical discourse were largely irrelevant. I felt very upset by this reaction, and realized it was because I had seen my role as their advocate, defending their rights. It was at this point that I began to understand my persistent tendency to study situations from the perspective of all those in subordinate roles, irrespective of whether they happened to be teachers or not. It was apparent in my work on the Ford Teaching Project, where hypotheses about classrooms were generated from the pupils' perspective. Looking back now I recognize this tendency in all the PLS case studies. In the study of Wynne's negotiations with LEAS, I looked at the negotiations from the LEAs' perspective. When I studied Schools Council decision making I looked at things from Wynne's perspective. Finally, when I looked at LEA personnel relating to teachers I tended to do so from the latter's perspective. The perspective I adopted was relative to the hierarchical structure of the situation.

Just before producing the final draft of the LEA conferences study I happened to read Harold Becker's 'Whose Side Are We On?' (in Filstead, 1970). Becker argues that social researchers cannot avoid studying a hierarchically structured situation from someone's perspective. He goes on to say that researchers are normally only accused of bias by those in superordinate roles when they adopt the perspective of the underdog. When researchers adopt the superordinate's perspective they are deemed to be unbiased. Becker accounts for this in terms of hierarchy of credibility. He writes:

> In any system of ranked groups, participants take it as given that members of the highest group have the right to define how things really are...Thus, credibility and the right to be heard are differentially distributed through the ranks of the system.

The article helped me to develop my thinking about the connection between the principle of justice and my role as 'the underdog's advocate'.

Triangulation

Although the 'underdog's advocate' stance does not involve accepting 'the underdog's' beliefs and opinions it does involve treating them seriously. Thus the researcher needs to enter into dialogue with subordinates as well as superordinates in order to test his hypotheses about, or interpretations and explanations of, the latter's conduct. In 'From Project to L.E.A.s Parts I and II' I attempted this by asking the LEA representatives present at the conference to respond to both my account of the proceedings and the Project Director's reply. Each party in 'the triangle' - researcher, Project Director, conference members - then had access to all three accounts in the form of a report which documented the discussion between the researcher and the other two parties. This procedure was also adopted in the study of Schools Council decision making.

Ideally such reports would go through a number of drafts as the researcher incorporated the responses to each in subsequent editions, thereby documenting an on-going debate. Constraints on time however made it only possible to produce a first edition incorporating all three accounts.

An alternative procedure is for the researcher to interview the subordinates and superordinates before making his own account accessible to them in a document which presents all three accounts. With the release of this document the discussion begins. This technique is the form of triangulation we used in the Ford Teaching Project. The researcher interviewed the teacher and his pupils before making the three points of view available to all three parties. It is important when adopting this version of triangulation procedures for the researcher to produce his account immediately after observation (from notes and recordings made during it) and before interviewing. Otherwise he is unable to test his own observation-based account against those of the participants.

One of the problems of using the triangulation technique I primarily adopted in this study - of gathering participants' perceptions by asking them to react to my own account - is that the critical nature of the researcher's account generates an over-defensive reaction, which can be avoided by eliciting participants' accounts prior to the release of the researcher's own. The hostile tone of some of the replies I received from LEA representatives began to convince me that I should have adopted the alternative technique used in the Ford Project. However, I gathered from informal conversations with people that 'the public defence' did not always express 'the private view' which emerged from participants' reflections on my analysis of conference events. This suggests that although the technique did not always elicit honest accounts it did have the effect of helping people to entertain privately alternative interpretations of events to their own, and thereby to reflect more deeply and systematically about their own and other people's conduct in the situation.

Critical Theory and Self-monitoring

This brings me to the function of critique in social research. Participants would frequently accuse me of paying too much attention to problems in people's conduct and not enough to its positive aspects. My response was generally to stress the role of critique in the development of self-monitoring ability, i.e. the ability to adopt an unbiased attitude towards one's own conduct. In order to adopt an unbiased attitude one needs to entertain alternative interpretations of one's conduct to the kind one will normally tend to give, i.e. interpretations which present it in a favourable light. This does not mean that one must always come to see one's own conduct in an unfavourable light, but that one ought at least to entertain the possibility that it is not as it seems. So for me critical hypotheses, regardless of their validity, have an important role to perform in fostering the self-monitoring competence of participants, particularly of those in superordinate roles. This was the function of 'the outsiders' research in the Ford Teaching Project; namely, to help teachers adopt a research attitude to their own conduct in the classroom. But during that Project I was not so clear about the status of 'the outsiders' research hypotheses as I am now. It now seems to me that the value of his hypotheses lies not so much in their truth as in their ability to foster self-reflection in participants. This recognition came about as a result of realizing that much of the hostility my interpretations generated in participants was based on the assumption that I was asserting truths rather than making conjectures. I tried to redress what I felt to be a misunderstanding of my intentions in the introduction to the final draft of the report on the conferences for LEA representatives.

It is normally assumed that the task of evaluation is to present a disinterested and unbiased account of events. On this assumption the evaluator's views are expected to carry greater authority than those of the major participants in the situation. The execution and presentation of this study is based on a rejection of this autocratic view of evaluation. We assume that the evaluator is as liable to bias as any other party simply because he, like the other participants, cannot avoid adopting some theory into which he will attempt 'to fit' the facts of the situation. It is his commitment to this theory which inevitably results in some degree of bias. A totally unbiased evaluator would be one who could observe the 'naked facts' of the situation and build his theory out of them. But the existence of 'naked facts' is a myth. All our observations are determined by our expectations and interpretative categories. The only way we can step outside our interpretative blinkers and criticize our own constructions of reality is to entertain alternative interpretative categories and the view of events they suggest.

It seems to me that a critique which fosters self-reflection leaves the question of its validity for the participants to answer. This is why in the reports I have ensured that my account preceded those of participants. In other words I let the participants have 'the last word'.

Formative Research/Evaluation

From the beginning of the dissemination study I saw the development of self-monitoring competence as a form of in-service education for

in-service educators. I have worked on the assumption, as we did
in the Ford Teaching Project, that the best way to improve practice
lies not so much in trying to control people's behaviour as in helping
them to control their own by becoming more aware of what they are doing.
On the basis of self-awareness people are in a position to control their
own behaviour and develop the necessary skills, because self-awareness is
a necessary condition to autonomous action. Thus programme and course
development takes place when people self-monitor their own practice. This
view of programme development makes the participation of in-service personnel in research and evaluation a central feature of their own in-service
development, and the research/evaluation conducted by 'outsiders' the
central formative influence on that development.

In accordance with this view of formative research/evaluation the PLS dissemination study involved the speedy production of interim working documents
on various aspects of the programme which could then be fed back to in-
service personnel during the actual course of the programme itself. These
documents were also made available to in-service personnel disseminating
the Project concurrently outside the trial areas. They included some of
the case studies already cited and a number of 'Reports from Schools'.
The latter largely consisted of self-evaluations by heads and staff involved
in school-based courses. The idea of these reports was both to encourage
self-evaluation and to provide schools with access to each others' experience.

For formative research and evaluation, speedy production and release of reports is essential. This means one has to compromise on rigour and polished
presentation in order to meet the requirements of action. This was difficult for some members of the Schools Council's staff to accept; they were
anxious about 'unfinished', provisional materials being widely available
in case their purpose was misunderstood and reflected badly on the work of
the Council.* As a result I am expected to control the release of working
documents so that they are made available to disseminators and researchers
rather than the widest possible audience. Given the formative aim of the
study I am not entirely unhappy with this arrangement, although as I shall
now try to argue, it is not ideal.

Democratic Research/Evaluation

Inasmuch as values like justice and freedom are central to the methodology
of the study I could not be neutral with respect to the distribution of
information about the programme. Such values define a democratic way of
life and as such it is in the public's interest to have information about
the extent to which they are being protected and fostered in various contexts. Democratic evaluation in general involves a commitment to free
information flow on matters which are relevant to the public interest. And

---

*
I have been asked to amplify this statement, which has been seen as incomplete.
The anxiety was felt by the Project consultative committee as well as Council
staff, and concerned the way in which early drafts transcribing spontaneous
conversation might give uninformed readers a misleading impression of teachers
and other participants and of the Project, rather than simply of the Council's
work.

this means that as much information should flow down social hierarchies as up them. Such procedures are bound to encounter difficulties. Information about others gives power over others and a more equal distribution of power involves a restructuring of social relations.

By about a year into the PLS study, however, I realized that one could make a distinction between information which is relevant to people as members of the public and that which is relevant to them as members of a particular group, because one could in fact define the notion of 'the public interest' in terms of democratic values. Thus democratic evaluation can be described as a form of evaluation which provides information relevant to the public interest rather than purely sectional interests. As such it cannot avoid judgement because it has to assess situations in the light of democratic criteria like justice and freedom.

The compromise I was asked to make by the Council was about the release of information. One of the problems about information release is that people may misuse the information they have access to. Instead of using information to improve the quality of in-service processes they may use it to promote their own personal and sectional interests in ways which harm the in-service personnel involved. The democratic evaluator has a responsibility to protect participants against information misuse. And this may mean totally denying some people access to the information. Hence, in retrospect, I do not think the Council was necessarily unwise in suggesting a compromise as it did. However, before one gets to the point of denying access completely there are other 'protection' procedures.

One strategy I adopted for protecting participants was to give them control over what was to be released. I now realize this is rather inconsistent with the idea of democratic evaluation, because people are given the freedom to withhold information it may be in the public's interest to know. However, in the absence of other procedures for protecting participants against harm it may be necessary. It also became necessary during the course of the study for the evaluator to exercise some control over release himself. The participants may not be aware of all the possible effects of release and the evaluator should at least point out those he is aware of if he thinks they are not being taken into account. It is only too easy to allow one's desire to get information released to override one's duty to protect participants from possible misuses.

Research and its Object

It remains for me to say something about the connection between the methodology which has emerged and the object of research/evaluation; namely, in-service teacher education. The methodology is grounded in views about the rights of participants - both in-service personnel and teachers - within the in-service process. With respect to teachers their freedom to enter into critical discourse and have their views treated justly is fundamental. With respect to in-service personnel their right to self-determine their own conduct in the light of self-reflection is fundamental. The task of research/evaluation in my view is to protect and enable the exercise of these rights so that in-service processes become genuinely educational. I assume that the concept of education is an evaluative one and defines a worthwhile form of process irrespective of the outcomes of that process. The methodology I have outlined is not dependent on the specification of product outcomes and suggests an alternative paradigm to protect orientated research/evaluation.

The criteria for assessing in-service processes are I believe implicit in the processes themselves and need not be derived from specifications of outcomes. In-service activities essentially consist of acts of communication. Refusal to enter into dialogue with one's audience and to give them critical access to one's views is a denial of the values implicit in acts of communication and indicative of distortion (including the denial of one's capacity for self-reflection).

Now I would argue that in order to be true to the phenomenon being studied research into in-service activities must necessarily view the constituent communication processes in the light of this supposition of accountability to those on the receiving end. The research will be trying to detect and explain cases of distorted communication in which teachers are denied the rights of dialogue and critical access. Such a situation constitutes an unjust state of affairs which is inconsistent with the presuppositions underlying the act of communication itself. Hence 'just treatment to the views of teachers' is a value position implicit in the nature of in-service activities. Research into such activities cannot remain true to 'the phenomenon' unless this commitment structures observations and the generation of hypotheses.

Chapter Six

A LOCAL EDUCATION AUTHORITY'S EVALUATION OF IN-SERVICE WORK

Evaluation as part of local authority in-service provision

The county of Suffolk in the extreme east of England provides an example of advanced evaluation practice as an integral part of local authority course structure. In the northern area of that county, over seven years, and more intensively in the last five, Chris Saville, a senior adviser, and his colleagues have been investigating and developing evaluation techniques. Saville's own account of this work is in preparation.

They see 'evaluation' as being not only necessary for the success and improvement of their courses but also as an important, indeed essential, message to be communicated to the heads and teachers with whom they work. The open and comprehensive techniques they employ are intended to show that those who teach must be responsible, accountable and responsive to those for whom the courses are provided. The development of evaluative skills and techniques as tools of classroom power for teachers to use to legitimize classroom knowledge (Saville's expression) is a main aim of their in-service work. The evaluation of in-service courses is seen as the way into promoting greater teacher responsibility and acceptable teacher-evaluation of work within schools.

A range of the techniques described elsewhere in this book is employed, since different uses and aims have been identified, but in reviewing techniques Saville is quite clear that critical descriptions of courses which avoid value judgement and are turned into intellectual exercises are not useful, and neither are evaluation reports which consist largely of long series of descriptions, interviews and participants' comments. Directions for development and value judgements need to be clearly and relatively concisely indicated if a report is to be of use, and for this the services of an external, paid, evaluator may be sought. The tape recording of discussions has been given up as too time-consuming; observation and listening approaches, without overt note-making, are recommended, since it is felt that recording alters what is said. Saville himself puts a high value on 'hear-say' evidence and relevant material which crops up, often when other quite different matters are being discussed. The processes now employed may be best introduced by a description of how they have been developed over the past five years, starting from a paper written by this senior adviser, a paper which questioned the validity, function and purpose of in-service activities and concluded that teachers should be made the buyers of in-service education. Such ideas permeated the thinking of those promoting subsequent in-service courses in the area.

North Suffolk first of all used conventional questionnaire forms which gave immediate information about course acceptability but they found, as most of us do, that responses were skewed towards the 'favourable' ends of scales and that the questions asked were, all too often, not those that seemed most relevant to those responding. It was decided that no 'all-purpose' form could be suitable since its use might predetermine course presentation and that something new would need to be planned for each course. The ingredients would usually involve statements ('underline the most appropriate phrases'), room for comments after each statement, and five or ten point scales to be completed (with almost predictable results). Statements used for a course for newly-qualified teachers, for example included:

'Underline the most appropriate phrases:

A. The course was a waste of time
    The course contained some useful parts
    The course did not focus on my problems
    The chance to meet colleagues was useful and I learned
     a lot from them
    The course was useful

B. I would have liked other topics
    There wasn't enough time spent on each topic
    I would have liked more discussion time
    I would have liked less discussion time
    The topics were useful and practical
    The topics were insufficiently practical

D. The school visits were a waste of time
    It was useful to see another school but I didn't learn much
    The school visit focussed my attention on organisational
     problems and helped me to sort out my own
    I learned a lot from my visit
    I would have preferred a school more like my own
    There was insufficient pre-visit guidance
    There was sufficient pre-visit guidance

F. Please mark the course on a 10 point scale for:-
    a) content
    b) method
    c) visit
    d) discussion

Later examples would probably have put the phrases in more continuous form or, for discussion sessions, have asked simple questions, but at this stage it became necessary to distinguish between forms intended for 'audit' purposes and those which would be more 'formative'. There can often be some confusion in thinking if one form is used for both purposes since that immediate evidence of the success or acceptability of a course which is needed for presentation to working parties or employers may be quite different from that which is truly 'developmental'. In addition to the 'statement and comment' therefore, a rapid assessment form was developed for audit purposes on which features of courses were to be rated A B C D E, with A being described as 'much above average'. Among the features listed were:

Organization: programme structure
Organization: presentation
Content: interest
Content: relevance
Documentation
Participation
Group discussions
Stimulation of thought
Stimulation of self-examination

It will be noted that the last two of these features represent key aims of the courses provided, and while the value of this form in general is considered rather limited, it is satisfactory that they have recently been so highly rated. It is suggested, incidentally, that course organizers should not design forms like this themselves, the one quoted was drawn up in consultation with the warden of the teachers centre where the course was to be held. An example of the latest form to be used is given at the end of the chapter.

It was considered a major step forward when the local authority agreed to the appointment of a paid external evaluator to report upon, in the first instance, a course for heads of departments in secondary schools. This evaluator, Mike Hayhoe, of Keswick Hall College of Education, was to act as participant observer and his report, which was to take the form of an open letter to the advisers responsible, was to focus on issues such as the values of the strategies and method of briefing and presentation.

The evaluator was introduced quietly and reassuringly to course members at the start (it may be best for the evaluator to introduce himself and his role) and sat in on subsequent sessions and social gatherings. Not until the end of the course, to avoid their becoming 'event-conscious', did he approach six individuals selected to form a representative sample of course members, and ask them to send him a tape or letter about the course. These were to be used anonymously and openly: it later proved that waiting for them delayed the report considerably. The report was found very valuable in giving the participant's view of reception and documentation, for example, in its tactful handling of criticisms of presentation and its highlighting of group reactions. It has led to more emphasis being placed on pre-course preparation. Even the introduction to the course was in future to be written beforehand, and files of documents were to be prepared to be given to participants on arrival.

As a result of these experiences a course for headteachers, run by the senior adviser and his colleagues, and designed to develop reflective skills, could be seen to have six evaluation components, three of which have been dealt with so far:

1. An external evaluator, paid, acting as participant observer and presenting a report. (That there are suitable evaluators available in this part of the country reflects the seminal work done by the local institute of education and especially by John Elliott, referred to elsewhere). This external evaluator also has a consultative role during the course and meets the course directors at the end of each day to discuss highlights of the day's work.

2. A rapid assessment form (anonymous).

3. Each of the organizers writes an account of his feelings, opinions and recommendations at the end of the course, giving his own criticisms from the aims of the course onwards (a part of evaluation also found important in the Northumberland Induction Scheme and commented upon earlier).

4. Visits to participants to see the effects of the course. Primary school headteachers who attended this course, for example, are now going ahead in their own schools with research projects based on what they have learned, and particularly upon the example set by the evaluative attitudes demonstrated. The effectiveness and interest they show as well as the degree to which they have adopted principles such as accepting criticism or realizing that 'you never find out the truth' are thought to be fair indications of the effectiveness of the course.

5. Informal references to the course's influences are looked for in all sorts of contexts and found to be most valuable (for example, an assistant teacher's 'My God, what have you done to our head' was both telling and succinct).

6. All those involved in running courses find that the constant emphasis upon evaluation as both process and theme has honed their perceptions of course members reactions and needs to a fine edge, so that all their reactions and interventions become more incisive (but not more cutting...)

This most promising evaluation procedure, the aim of which is no less than the reform of school organization through altering the whole pattern and hierarchy of curriculum change, with teacher evaluators as the gatekeepers of innovation, naturally has problems and difficulties and provokes numerous questions. Some of these are considered in the next paragraphs. They seem to centre round a recognition that evaluation is rather a habit of mind or deep seated attitude than merely a collection of techniques, and before it can be accepted it is necessary to dispel doubts about the threatening aspects of either the processes or persons involved. Evaluation has to be seen as a game which when properly played enhances rather than threatens the individual teacher's self-esteem.

In the first instance there is the problem of who should see evaluation reports, and to what extent the external evaluator's report should become the 'open' property of the LEA. We have already noted that different forms of report are needed on different occasions, but when it comes to, for example, a report from an external evaluator should it go to all course members? This problem was raised in an interesting form during a conference when the headteachers present felt they should all see the evaluation report on that conference, although when it came to the question of who should see reports on the evaluation of their own schools, they at first insisted that these should be confidential and seen only by themselves - a natural reaction in the present teaching situation.

This leads directly to the question of how an external evaluator should be chosen. That he needs to have suitable skills, experience and expertise is clear, but should he be chosen by the course organizers on the grounds that they 'know his work, like his style and have confidence in him'? It is believed that, as is the case when picking external examiners, these are indeed sufficient grounds for choice since the organizers then know that while they must be under examination they do not feel threatened by that knowledge.

That evaluation is often perceived as a potential threat becomes clear during discussion with teachers and the preservation - indeed enhancement - of their self-esteem is a difficulty facing both evaluators and those presenting courses on evaluation. In the long run the development of evaluation skills and attitudes among teachers themselves, so that they can both give and accept criticism in the proper context and become used to a more 'open' professional atmosphere is the answer, but in the meantime it is important that the sense of threat be kept down to a stimulating level rather than to one of fear of failure. It is suggested that an approach which encourages teachers is to stress that it is important that they should themselves be familiar with and control evaluation techniques rather than have them imposed from outside. The fact that the courses and procedures dealt with here are organized and often run by LEA advisers is itself a difficulty, which they well appreciate. They may be leaders in a teacher-based movement but they are also seen as authority figures - perhaps even more to heads than to new teachers.

Two further difficulties experienced by these advisers in presenting and carrying out evaluation programmes should be mentioned. A teacher coming into a course all too often expects there to be appropriate and acceptable answers to the questions he is asked. This is often not the case where evaluation is concerned. Questions may be asked which turn out to be unanswerable and teachers need to be convinced that what is needed is for them to think naturally, searchingly and responsibly about what is being done. This is not always an easy idea to pass on, nor are evaluation concepts in general. Approaches such as these tend to be presented and recommended by those of us who have come a good way along the evaluation path. There is a temptation for us to try to over-accelerate teacher's progress along that path. Experience in Suffolk and elsewhere emphasizes the need to proceed with caution.

Equally, the care, concern, commitment and sheer amount of work involved in promoting a developing programme such as Saville's must be emphasized. And while in some ways the scheme once established becomes easier to run, in others it becomes harder, because more deep-rooted developments are seen to be needed. So in the last two years work done earlier, especially in the form of research agendas and findings, have been used in courses to raise standards and form a second generation of work in the field. It has been possible also to develop a series of pre-course interviews to monitor teachers' expectations for the guidance of tutors and to afford comparison with course outcomes.

But it is seen that the ultimate outcomes, improvements in schools consequent upon what has been done in the in-service programme, depend upon the schools being prepared for these changes and developments. The answer would seem to be to arrange school-based in-service work to create the

basic enabling conditions in schools. So a circular condition is seen to
be necessary and the whole external course/in-school development must be
interdependent because the effectiveness of each depends on the other.
Saville points out that this enabling and preparative function is also
necessary where in-service work is to be school-focused when an outside
agent is involved. The programme in Suffolk therefore has led to a major
move into school-based developments. In much the same way as the acceptance of evaluation is best brought about by teaching about evaluation, so
the way to the acceptance and appreciation of in-service professional
development is through its introduction in schools - an important but not
simple development.

Chapter Seven

TWO STUDIES ARISING FROM THE EVALUATION OF THE TEACHER INDUCTION PROJECT

(a)   The Evaluation of Teachers' Centres and School-based Activities

John Davis, University of Liverpool

Note

This case study is very different from those which precede it in both style and aims. It focuses on in-service activities which are at a less developed stage than earlier examples and illuminates the exploratory steps taken towards effective evaluation.

The evaluator was drawn into this exploration through his involvement in the Teacher Induction Pilot Scheme, but his report has wider applications in local authority activities. Much of it is illustrated by quotations from discussions between the evaluator (EV.) and a member of the staff of a teachers' centre (G.).

Interests and relationships

In the context of the Induction Pilot Scheme it was clearly part of the local evaluator's brief to monitor and draw conclusions about the work of the seven professional centres in Liverpool, for national as well as local consumption. Whilst it was to be hoped that the centres would also become better able to evaluate for themselves it was left to individual centres to decide the extent to which they would undertake additional evaluation activities. Apart from the work of the evaluator, which was of course available to them, for most centres evaluation remained an informal process left mainly to individual course tutors. Two centres, and in particular the Liverpool Teachers' Centre (LTC), took it more seriously. The LTC had been using questionnaires before induction, and in any case the situation with a small number of staff working closely together was probably more amenable to discussion of procedures, findings and subsequent decision making. There were several pressures to evaluate:

> From the induction evaluator, for participation in monitoring the Centre's work with the probationers.

> From the LTC Advisory (i.e. management) Committee, to demonstrate that the Centre was working effectively.

> Internally, themselves as the staff who organized (but not necessarily ran) the courses.

G. It's a difficult one. I think it cropped up at a staff
meeting that we had some time ago that there was a need to
evaluate courses. We weren't quite sure why people were
coming on courses, we weren't sure about the success of courses -
what effect the courses were having on teachers and, therefore,
the kind of evaluations we were doing, which weren't particularly brilliant, we thought about amending and revising.

The staff at the Centre took no decision to work on evaluation or to dele-
gate to any person the job of considering it further but there was con-
census that it was necessary and one of them (G) took it upon himself to
do something about it. He was studying part-time for BEd at a college
of education, but said he took the work on partly for his own career,
partly because he was likely to have time on his hands next year (there
were to be five Junior probationers only for induction) and because he
felt it was needed. He sought guidance from a colleague at another
teachers' centre, who turned up an article by a teachers' centre warden
on the evaluation of in-service education courses:

G. She was doing an MEd and had come across this article. We
talked about evaluation and some of the problems that we would
have to face and she was writing an essay and had come across
this article. But he was looking towards some kind of taxonomy
of objectives and seeing the make up of the course and also the
degree to which the course had actually met those objectives.
I was a bit confused. I don't know whether it was a good idea
and R. (the Induction Coordinator at the Centre) had mentioned
that you were doing evaluation of the induction, so the contact
was there.

The evaluator was interested in becoming involved and took care in developing the association - establishing relationships and building credibility
with all Centre staff through increased contact, socializing over lunch,
at the pub and through induction activities. He played squash with G. and
R. and spent some time discussing the potentials and problems of evaluation,
obtaining commitment and elements of an informal contact with these two,
but not to any great extent with other Centre staff. Nevertheless G.
would now be under further pressures to evaluate, from this relationship,
from his colleagues seeing that he had taken up the initiative, and from
the Chief Inspector and the Director of Education, who, on a visit to the
Centre, had said that he would support it to the hilt.

What to evaluate

Previous practice for all courses was to record attendances and ask all
course members to complete a standard questionnaire which involves rating
(on a 2 or 3 point scale) and comment on each of the following points for
the course as a whole:

1. Aims - were the aims set out on the programme achieved?
    Were your specific needs met?

2. Content - was the topic treatment advanced/elementary? Was
    the content relevant or not?

3. Methods - was the course long/short? Did the course relate to the classroom? Did the course relate to the teaching situation? How satisfied were you with equipment and literature?

4. Administration - how satisfied were you with catering? Accommodation? Organized visits etc.?

5. Overall rating on a 5 point scale.

Some, but not all, course descriptions specified aims and (behavioural) objectives, e.g. Social/Environmental Studies 9 - 13.

AIM: to examine issues and define principles which guide the formulation of an individual social/environmental studies curriculum.

OBJECTIVES: at the end of the course it is hoped that course members will be able to:-

1. outline an individual social/environmental studies programme;

2. identify issues connected with social/environmental studies;

3. define principles to guide the formulation of a social/ environmental studies programme;

4. define skill-building in relation to child-development;

5. objectively examine and evaluate personal and published social/environmental studies programmes. ·

Bearing in mind that LTC staff organize courses but do not necessarily teach on them, G.'s initial inclinations were to improve the questionnaire, perhaps by incorporating sections asking whether particular aims and objectives had been met, and to use these sections as a basis for improving discussions between Centre staff and course tutors about what they hoped the course would achieve, and how it would do so. Nevertheless G. was considering a standard format, to be used for all courses, for the purpose of making comparisons between them.

In considering what questions needed to be asked discussion between G. and the evaluator inevitably shifted to an exploration of the purposes of evaluation, providing vital clarification of problems facing the Centre staff, which evaluation or the evaluator might be expected to help deal with. It became apparent, for instance, that the LTC staff felt a need to justify themselves to their 'masters', of whom there are several. Resource provision is controlled by the administrators in the Education Office, in terms of Centre finances and staff salaries, since it is to them (Teacher Development Section) that teachers apply to attend the courses. The Centre used to be managed by a committee:

G. Historically there used to be four management committees
who had direct powers over the four units of the Centre, those
days have now gone. People from the management committee have
now found themselves in an advisory capacity, and they are
unsure about their precise role and the control they have over
the Centre...they are in a great quandary at the moment whether
they are, in fact, a management committee or an advisory committee. Their role is being clarified by the Director but there
are still ambiguities.

EV. And what did the Director decide?

G. That the committee should be advisory and therefore feed in
information to the Centre which would be of use in planning
courses and projects.

EV. And how do they see themselves? Do they see themselves as
experts, going along to give their opinions?

G. Yes.

EV. Do they see it as pondering over your evaluations and trying to decide things like philosophy and rationale and procedures of training and in-service?

G. I don't think they see it at that level, they see it far more
as a surface thing. They will say it is going well, therefore
it could be repeated.

The Advisory Committee comprises the Chief Inspector, advisors - including
one who has special responsibility for the work of the Centre - Centre
staff and a number of practising teachers. These tend mainly to be union
representatives:

G. therefore, the Committee is seen to be democratic. You have
teacher representatives on the Committee and, therefore, the bulk
of Liverpool teachers are represented.

The Centre has other masters in the sense that it serves the various people
who want either to run their own course there, or who suggest or commission
the Centre staff to run courses for them:

EV. How did most of your courses get established? Who decides
there will be a course in this and sets about planning it?

G. It's very much left to the individual officers in the Centre,
but there are a whole series of influences. The advisers will
say there ought to be a course of Science 5 - 13 and will we put
it into operation - there are a lot of initiatives, hopefully,
taken up by officers in the Centre. One of the big problems is
the kind of communication that exists between the office, the
Centre and the schools. Again there are so many representatives
of the voice of the teachers that you are torn in different
directions. You could go, for instance, to the Advisory Committee

and ask them for suggestions for courses but the suggestions
that they make will, in fact, be a particular interest that
they have and may not be representative of all in this field.
Again in the office the advisers may suggest a course in a
particular field, not because that has been suggested to them
in school, but because they have an interest. There are so
many inputs that you begin to wonder which are the most valid.

In expressing dissatisfaction with the *ad hoc* way in which courses are
generated it would seem that LTC staff do not view themselves merely as
a service agency, but take a professional concern over in-service provision by trying to ensure that any gaps left by the several 'commissioning
agents' are met by their own initiatives. To some degree their positions
are dependent on being able to drum up sufficient business, but there is
an underlying uncertainty about how far they have a mandate to do so when
they also have to service other people's requests and requirements. In
the absence of clear criteria from others they may well be seeking through
evaluation a means of identifying and obtaining confirmation of criteria
by which their own policies may be directed. It was also clear that the
Centre staff were genuinely concerned to try to get behind the assumptions
that were usually made about courses in order to provide what they thought
was needed - even if nobody seemed to be requesting it.

G. In the first place, if we simply ask which sessions have been
successful and which have failed it seems to suggest that we
are just looking for refinement of that course and the assumption is, therefore, that that course is valuable. What we are
trying to do is to look back at the stage before that and to ask
if the course is valuable, whatever that means. It is not just
'Do teachers want to come on the course?' - that is relatively
easy to measure - you just tick off people as they come through
the door. But it's the real value and impact of the course
which is puzzling because again it is a personal thing and it
has become such a difficult thing to get to grips with that we
simply made assumptions that we think, or an adviser thinks, or
whoever thinks, that a particular course is valuable and, therefore, it will be put on. People come along to the course and
that seems to justify it.

Such expressions of doubt are probably nothing new to the Centre staff,
but this in itself points to a further problem, that the Centre's present
machinery for identifying and solving problems is somewhat ineffective -
mostly the staff meet informally and produce little in the way of tangible
definitions of difficulties or prescriptions for action. That doesn't
mean that new methods were not tried out, but it suggests that these were
somewhat isolated, individual initiatives and that results were rarely presented as part of a clear decision making procedure. It appears that G.'s
written reports on induction courses were the first such reports that had
been produced:

EV. How much influence has induction had on you getting down
to making evaluation reports?

G. Very much because there has been a lot of energy there, it has also been a fairly precise, well thought out programme with a specific number of people who are in weekly contact with the Centre which makes evaluation that much easier. We are not getting people zooming off somewhere else and never crossing the threshold again. We have got continuous contact.

After discussions with the evaluator it was agreed that G. would focus on two aspects - firstly looking in greater depth at a number of courses in order to identify areas of difficulty in planning and organization and to determine which parts of the courses were/were not successful. Secondly, in the light of current interest in school-based in-service work, he was to look at certain courses that the Centre was about to mount in schools, to see what could be learned from the experiences.

Evaluating the courses, and some consequences

The evaluator had written a summary of discussions as a general background, mentioning matters such as tutor and course member expectations, course transactions and outcomes and need for views from others besides the consumers, but the sample questionnaire that G. produced for inspection suggested that the 'tutorial' discussions were not well understood. The questionnaire was an expanded version of the earlier single sheet, asking similar questions but for each session rather than for the course as a whole, and for all but the induction courses no other procedure was used and no other protagonists were asked for their views. There was something of a hurry and as the evaluator didn't wish either to formulate the questionnaire on G.'s behalf or to start at the beginning again, he didn't interfere. From time to time the evaluator inquired about how things were going, and interviewed and took notes from G. and R. partly for induction purposes and partly to ensure that the background was on record. Towards the end of the year G. experienced difficulty in dealing with the considerable data he had accumulated, and asked the evaluator to discuss what might go into a report. It was clear that G. understood what the questionnaires indicated about individual sessions, and could identify which were the useful questions and numerical data; in part the difficulty was that he was trying to read too much into the data and this may well have been an attempt to tackle the various things covered in earlier discussions - perhaps to meet the expectations of the evaluator. After confirming G. in his conclusions, suggesting other questions to ask of the data and discussing who the report was for and the need to write different reports aimed at different people, G. was left to write up his findings. The first draft was very successful, which may mean that having to sort out ideas on paper stimulated the real learning here, and after suggesting a few structural changes and some further comparisons, the evaluator left whistling contentedly to himself. The report. and its conclusions, were discussed at a staff meeting, to which the evaluator was invited but could not attend:

> G. At the beginning of the meeting I was trying to explain that they ought to make decisions, and that in the light of the evaluation there were some decisions that could be made even though the evaluation might not be entirely satisfactory. The meeting structured itself - they started off talking about the general findings and then it was suggested that they move towards looking

at each course separately. This was very useful because the
general points were repeatedly coming through and being
emphasized, and people were seeing them in a context. The
general points were such things as vagueness. Courses were
planned very vaguely and the intentions behind the course were
not thought through. 'Needs...' is just a term which is used,
but nobody thinks about planning to find out what teachers'
needs are. One of the decisions it was hoped to make was how
to go about finding what teachers' needs are, and to build a
strategy for doing so.

One of the matters on which discussion focused was a visit by probationary
teachers to Colomendy, the LEA field centre. There were clear differences
of opinion as to the value of this trip: some said it was useful to see
the place, others said it wasn't relevant, either because a probationer had
other priorities at that time or because business studies teachers (for
instance) would be unlikely to need to use it. These differences of opinion
reflected a fundamental difficulty of evaluation for them, which concerned
the problem of planning a course (i.e. deciding what goes in or not) in
the face of the substantially disparate values different people place on
different items. Similarly, staff were also concerned about the problems
of trying to plan a course to meet the different needs of the various
people who would be attending.

Potentially, this impasse represents a make or break situation for the
future of LTC evaluation. While the bridge must derive from the determina-
tion of the staff to do something constructive about the problem rather
than from what the evaluation has to offer, it seems inevitable that the
evaluator or some other influential person intervene to suggest what needs
to be done and to confirm the usefulness of doing it. What is at stake
here is the decision making or problem solving capability of the Centre
staff. A further difficulty lies in whether they appreciate what the evaluation has shown them, or not; and this appreciation requires a certain
amount of insight and awareness which they haven't yet been able to supply
for themselves even though their usual subjective methods of evaluation
have almost certainly indicated the problems before now. As with the
teacher/learner relationship, and the supervisor/learner-teacher relationship, this seems to be a critical time when the necessary factors coincide
and the learning mileage can be gained - but only if somebody present has
the necessary knowledge to bridge the gap, and I guess that means the
'evaluator-as-Guru'. What the evaluation process can do, if it is sufficiently broad, is to put things down on paper and so prolong the period
when factors may coincide and anyone who reads it can suggest an answer
and confirm the value of making the effort. The creativity of the process,
as a science, lies in asking good questions. One question in G.'s report
'What do we want to know?' is in part the primary problem in any research
of knowing where to begin, and this needs to be informed by some structure
of knowledge and theory or at least some structuring of experience. In
part, though, it is also a plea for common purpose, for leadership perhaps. Is this what the evaluator is being asked to provide?

Evaluating the school-based experiences, and some consequences.

Since the courses held in the three junior schools were comparable to
centre-based courses, G. used the same questionnaire format, supplemented
by descriptions of discussions that he and R. had with the various people

concerned - as tape recorded conversations with the evaluator - and occasional written reports from school staff. Findings were summarized by G. in a report to LTC staff, which dealt with each school primarily in terms of teacher opinion about the course sessions, but went on to pose questions and draw conclusions that relate to the strategic implications, as points intended for discussion and hopefully also decisions:

1. That on visiting the school to discuss the notion of a school-based course the mention of existing centre-based courses may detract from the essence of school-based in-service, i.e. that specified needs can be met.

2. Needs must be discussed and stated so that the course can be designed to meet them.

3. Closer liaison between school and speakers needs to be encouraged if speakers are to make their lectures relevant.

4. The real involvement of teachers in each session should be encouraged and stated to each speaker in his brief.

5. The evaluation needs to be looked at more critically to provide better, more useful information and over a longer period. Record keeping needs to be made more efficient.

While to an outsider these summaries might need further amplification than the report provides, LTC staff may well know what is in G.'s mind. Point 1., and to some extent 2. and 3. concern the critical area of initiating in-service work in schools, and it is possible that Centre staff are well aware of the implication that their influence becomes potentially one of curriculum development rather than course organization. That is not to say that their clients have the same expectations.

In fact school-based courses have tended to be centre-style courses held in schools, but the underlying purposes have not necessarily been the same. The course at School B arose in the usual way, but had particular usefulness for the staff:

G. R., probably in the light of the Great Debate and the speeches that were made, especially in October, decided it was important for the Centre to be picking up the basics. He had been interested in maths and therefore thought the next basic to look at was English and started to think around a junior English course. The idea was bounced around for some time and we fed in snippets, and some ideas, but it was solely on R.'s shoulders that the course got off the ground. He met the adviser and organized some meetings to set up the course.

Advisers and Centre staff met on some three or four occasions:

G. Mostly to confirm who would be saying what and for how long. The first session planned out the course, the subsequent sessions looked at problems that were cropping up along the way, such as someone couldn't come along and who could we get in their place and so on.

Although details were given in the LEA Bulletin, School B knew that the course was impending through R.'s wife, who was a teacher (and a teacher-tutor) there.

> G. They leapt at the course, they were rewriting their schemes of work and saw this as a good opportunity of sitting down and finding some new ideas and useful information which might be fed into the scheme of work.

They were toying with the idea of sending one person to each session so that most of the staff could go along to the course, and in the Centre at the same time we had been talking about school-based courses and again that piece of information was fed by R. to his wife.

> EV. The Head was presumably in favour by that stage?

> G. Yes, talks had gone well between the Centre and the head and some members of staff, so when we went along the idea was not brand new, they had had time to prepare. We both went down for the morning, the head took the assembly and allowed us to have a good hour with the staff. We talked to them about the possibility of a school-based course and said, briefly, that the Centre could put on a general course and people will come, however, only some of what is said will apply to those people - but with a school-based course it can be geared more to the particular needs of the school. It won't be perfect but it will be closer than the general course and they were quite pleased about that. There were still some people who were very hesitant. We talked about content of the junior English course and what would be appropriate to them. In fact, we left it there and said 'Have a think about it, if any of these sessions are of use they can be included. Let us know which sessions you want, the times you want it and we will organize it for you', and the head had very kindly said the school could close from 3 PM one day per week. In fact, the course ran from 3 to 5, so some of the time was school time and some of the time was teachers' time. Some members of staff went at the stroke of 4 PM every session, post haste.

The 'Teaching Young Readers Course' at School A was initiated rather differently:

> G. It had been advertised, in fact the first session had been held, and it was decided that there were so many people who wanted to come to that course that it made sense to say that we would run a course at the school. We got back to them through the course organizer, who was all in favour of it. He and the remedial team work in the area so that they have the contacts in the school and it didn't seem to make a lot of sense for us drily saying there will be a course...when he could actually go into the school, look at the problems in the school, which they know intimately, and say 'If you want to know more about the solution to these problems we could include these in a particular session'.

The same course at School C was also arranged through the remedial team, but:

> G. It was a difficult situation, three schools were merging into one and the head wanted to see if it was possible to organize a course for all the staffs to come together. One spin-off would be the establishment of a reading policy. Some of the teachers didn't really consider it necessary. The course was loosely based around the 'Teaching of Young Readers' course, and there were only four sessions.

Another lesson was that these school-based courses could bring staff policies into the open:

> G. From the discussions beforehand (in School B) you could tell that some members of staff were not in favour of the course, and you could also tell this when they were on the course because, come 4 PM, off they would go. But that was a small minority. We were told through R.'s wife that the staff were split for and against the course, and this seemed to come across in the evaluation too, although most of the staff were very pro the course.
>
> EV. How did this arise?
>
> G. Possibly the personalities of the staff. Also during the planning particular people may not have been involved and they may have wanted to be. The main problem therefore seems to be being democratic about setting up the course, and to spot that these feelings exist, although it can't be that simple. Maybe we need to look for a different vehicle for communicating ideas, which is basically what the exercise was all about.

The Centre staff appreciate the need to spend time in schools discussing with heads and others how they can help, and the foregoing examples indicate that this needs to be approached with a certain amount of circumspection. There are two particular areas of concern: the first, that they may be usurping the advisers' functions of assessing in-service needs and initiating policies to cater for them, although the advisers recently carried out a survey, the results of which have so far not been communicated to Centre staff. Secondly, the existing method for justifying the work of the Centre is essentially that of attendance numbers, mainly because this is the sort of criterion that treasury departments deal in. Although some schools have thrown open their doors for others to attend 'their' course, in practice fewer people attend school-based courses than centre-based courses and it is inevitable that this will be so if the rationale for such courses is school-centred.

G. was confident that the course at School B had been more successful than most, and felt that subsequent work was an important outcome - but there were no attempts to continue the co-operation, perhaps because this hadn't been requested. I suspect that the notion of planning course activities in order to continue to work with the school staff would at present be considered as going beyond their brief, even as being rather subversive. It would appear that the LTC staff probably still see themselves as providing a service to those who have already identified a need, rather than as structurers of situations in which such needs can be identified and worked on together. The foundations for such a style of working are already present in the workshop activities and the 'linking' or 'knowledge broker' functions which derive from the knowledge the Centre staff have developed of local teacher expertise. Interestingly, in planning a training course for teacher tutors in induction, R. sees a need for intervention in the work of the teacher-tutor, and has identified ways in which this can be begun and maintained. The notion of training through the work the teacher is already engaged in may well spread to other centre staff, but even if such intervention is proved effective the centre still faces the problem of encouraging those others who teach on their courses to do the same. More of the potential difficulties of school-based work are mentioned in G.'s report than are listed above. One concerns the expectation that the school is able to state its problem, when in fact it may not have got beyond the stage where individual teachers are thinking of their own problems, the implication being that centre staff may need to encourage necessary procedures in school before a stage is reached when a course can be organized. G. felt strongly that the difficulties that had come to light needed further exploration, but was uncertain about how far the Centre staff could be seen (or would feel happy) to be questioning staff and taking notes, particularly after the event:

> G. I feel that we ought to be recording far more, and certainly I haven't been writing things down, but, while it is fine to get ideas from the school staff and then get people to come in and support and develop them, our role later on where we look at the effect of the course, is questionable. The staff of the school, perhaps, are the people to evaluate the course.

He went on to suggest (bless him) that some of these difficulties might be solved by involving an outsider in the evaluation. He also suggested that it was time that I came and talked to the Centre staff about what they might do next. I hope I didn't accept with undignified haste.

I wonder how they would react if I explained this model to them?

It would greatly assist us in the planning of future courses if you would fill in the details below -

COURSE TITLE ....

AGE RANGE TAUGHT   Secondary   Junior   Infant

---

1. COURSE AIMS	Completely	Fairly well	Not at all	COMMENTS
Did the Course achieve its aims as set out in the programme?				
Were your specific needs met?				

---

2. COURSE CONTENT	Too Advanced	About Right	Too elementary
Considering the Course title, was the level of topic treatment			
	Very Relevant	Fairly Relevant	Not at all Relevant
Was the content of the Course			

---

3. METHODS	Too Long	About Right	Too short
Was the Course	Completely	Fairly Well	Not at all
Did the course relate to the classroom situation?			
Did the Course relate to the teaching situation?			
	Satisfied	Not Satisfied	
How satisfied were you with equipment (visual aids etc.) literature, (handouts etc.)?			

---

4. ADMINISTRATION	Satisfied	Not Satisfied

(b)   *Evaluation of the Teacher Induction Pilot Schemes (TIPS)*
       Project: Some problems of a large-scale action research project
       Keith Baker, University of Bristol

Introduction

This article sketches the evaluation approach and some of the problems faced
by the evaluation team on the Teacher Induction Pilot Schemes (TIPS) Project. It is not written as an illustration of a research design or as a
recommended form of approach to an action project. It attempts a straightforward, non-technical account which it is hoped may be of use to administrators and others who become involved in large-scale research or evaluation
projects. They may not be too concerned with the technicalities but may need
to understand some of the major issues if they are to aid effective evaluation.

The present gap between education researchers, teachers and administrators
is too wide and needs to be narrowed. The problems of researchers need to
be portrayed for these other groups, and vice-versa, if we are all to come
to a more fruitful understanding and co-operation in the business of unravel-
ling the complexities of educational processes and education systems.

The Induction Schemes

Following recommendations in a government White Paper (Great Britain, DES,
1972), the DES funded two pilot induction schemes for probationers (beginning
teachers). These were mounted in Liverpool and Northumberland, had a preparation year, 1973-4, and commenced with the September 1974 probationers.

The main features of the schemes were: a reduced teaching load for probationers,
allowing one day per week for induction activities; the appointment of a member of the school staff as 'teacher-tutor' to assist the probationers in that
school, with extra pay and a time allowance for doing this work; in Liverpool
the creation of professional centres in the local colleges of education and
teachers' centre to mount external support activities for the probationers
during some of their release time; but in Northumberland, a large rural area,
external support was given mainly through residential block-release courses.

Originally five pilot schemes were planned, but, under the 1973 economic
constraints, only two were actually begun. These were in the city of Liverpool and the rural county of Northumberland. Local evaluators based in local
universities were appointed to each of these schemes[1] early in 1974, but the
negotiations to establish a central co-ordinating team based at the University
of Bristol School of Education Research Unit[2] were not concluded until the
Summer of 1974 and appointments were concluded in time to allow a start on
October 1, which was, in fact, the contractual start of the central team's
project. This central team was given a brief to promote, inform and co-ordinate
both the monitoring and dissemination aspects of the two pilot induction
schemes funded by the DES and also to survey other induction schemes being
developed by other LEAs but funded purely from their own resources[3].

A summary table showing the principal evaluation and dissemination activities at national and local level is given at the end of this study.

1.   SOME STARTING PROBLEMS

The local evaluators appointed for each scheme began to operate from early in 1974 but at this stage they had little contact and no agreed approach to the evaluation. The delay in appointing the central team meant that the action components of the scheme were underway in the Summer of 1974, with tutor-preparation courses, and in September with probationer induction meetings, before the full evaluation team was established. The collection of base-line data was seriously impaired by this situation and one can only stress that teams must be brought together with sufficient time to allow the development of evaluation instruments before, or at the beginning of, the action programme.

Immediate problems were the lack of sufficient comparable base-line data, differing approaches by the two local evaluators who had mapped out their own evaluation programmes, and the need for the central team to become thoroughly cognisant with the features, personalities and *modus operandi* of the local schemes. As a team we needed to agree on a conceptual framework for our approach to the evaluation, to decide the evaluation strategy at national and local level, co-ordinate the activities, questionnaire design, question formats and programmes of the local evaluators and to integrate this with evaluation activities centrally[4]. This is a retrospective rationalization, however; it certainly never seemed so tidy in our early evaluation meetings.

2.   EVALUATION IN YEAR I

We soon agreed that the existing local evaluation plans would continue with only slight modifications, but consultation over questionnaire framing would take place to ensure some comparability of data; that while we needed comparative data, we would also treat the rural and urban schemes as separate case studies which, among other things, would allow other LEAs considering adoption of the innovation to 'identify' and make their own comparisons; that we would study the schemes as complex innovation management decisions at many levels[5]; that in the first year the central team would concentrate upon studies on the introduction of the innovation into particular schools and conduct a survey of induction practices in other LEAs.

We did not reach such easy agreement about the criteria by which the schemes might be judged for their effectiveness. Our basic problem was how to measure the effects of an in-service activity comprising several disparate features, namely, a lightened teaching load, teacher-tutor support and arranged induction activities either in school or at external centres. All three of these elements were variable in themselves along many dimensions. Even if a variance in children's learning or probationer teaching could be established in any sort of 'before and after' study, how could this be shown to be related to the in-service activity per se? And to which part of that activity in particular? Clearly there were major problems of intervening variables, of suitable criteria for what constitutes effective teaching and of establishing any relevant alternation in children's learning which could

be said to result from these in-service activities undertaken by probationers in approximately six hours per week. These problems underlay a reluctance in the team to press for either longitudinal surveys of effects on
probationers or direct classroom observation.

But were we not to check for increased 'effectiveness' of probationers'
teaching? Not see if they were better teachers? Without answers on criteria such as these, how could we be said to be evaluating the induction
schemes? We concluded that we could not make measurements about the effectiveness of the probationers' teaching, since the research tools and criteria
for determining what is or makes for an effective teacher or effective
teaching are not sufficiently well established. In an early decision,
therefore, we ruled out any examination of children's learning and classroom assessment of the probationers' teaching.

This decision, coupled with the lack of comparable base-line data, made
the adoption of a classical research approach with before and after measures
rather difficult, especially for the first year, and we therefore adopted
a more anthropological approach, using 'illuminative' evaluation techniques.
The team was reluctant to completely forsake the classical approach and con-
stantly re-appraised the situation and our original decisions. Subsequently,
McCabe developed an 'Induction Attitude Scale' and even in the third year
of the evaluation, the team considered a plan to establish control groups
and obtain independent ratings of the probationers. This plan was eventually abandoned, partly through problems of getting control groups and
partly because we felt that the original objections still applied.

Our principal source of evidence about the schemes, then, has been the
opinions of the various groups involved. But several comments made during
interviews with various levels of participants suggested that we could hardly
rely on evidence from the major participants. It was said that those most
involved would be biased, since the tutors were receiving extra money and
the probationers had one day per week 'off' and would be bound to favour
this, while the organizers and administrators who were trying hard to
operationalize the scheme successfully would naturally be in its favour.
In fact, these allegations of bias did not appear to be borne out either
by the work of the local evaluators or by the first year intensive pilot
case studies in particular schools undertaken by the central team. The
probationers were not wholeheartedly in favour of the release, as some
teachers had suggested they would be, and certain groups, such as reception
class teachers, were rather against it. The administrators were very quick
to acknowledge 'teething' problems and to make alterations in the light of
their experience, and some of the tutors we studied said they did not want
the pay and did not think the work should be paid. Of course, there are
problems in interpreting the motives for and the efficacy of such remarks,
but they appeared to suggest that the simple allegations of bias were not
entirely to be believed. Judgements from earlier projects in this field
had also pointed to the use of the opinions of those involved as a legitimate and practical yardstick for assessing the schemes. The team resolved
to continue to regard the informed professional judgement of those involved
as a major source of evidence about the effectiveness and practicality of
the scheme.

3.   EVALUATION IN YEAR 2

We used the case studies, interviews and questionnaire data from our
studies in the first year as sensitizing data from which we derived a large

questionnaire, aimed at a wide cross-section of the school personnel involved. This was administered in January 1976, allowing opinions about the Christmas term induction to be expressed, and a much shorter questionnaire was then sent out to most of the respondents in June 1976, covering the Spring and Summer term induction programmes.

The central team interviewed most of the LEA advisers in Liverpool and Northumberland who had been involved in the scheme, using a semi-structured interview schedule. Similarly, interviews were held with a sample of staff from each of the 'professional centres' involved in the Liverpool scheme. These were based principally upon semi-structured interview schedules and provided supplementary data to questionnaires which had been administered by the local evaluators in the first year. In fact, the local evaluators' report had reflected strong consumer criticism of the external components of the induction scheme, and some changes in organization were made in response to such criticism.

A number of general issues relating to the evaluation team and its activities by this time may be raised. The first is the problem faced by the local evaluators of being, in effect, virtually independent field officers, but linked to the central evaluation team on the one hand and to the local scheme organizers on the other. As local evaluators, they had access to and attended meetings at every level of the scheme, e.g. professional centre age range working party, induction co-ordinators' meetings, professional centre meetings for heads, tutors and probationers, and the representative LEA Advisory Committee on Induction. They were, therefore, in close contact with the LEA advisory and administrative officers, who were organizing the scheme, and the professional centre co-ordinators who organized external activities for probationers, etc. In the first year, this had raised some doubts about the independence of the local evaluators in the eyes of teachers, and time had to be spent in establishing relationships and gaining credibility as an independent evaluator. But working closely with organizers, LEA advisers, professional centre principals and co-ordinators raises problems about the possible co-optation of the local evaluators into local value systems. It was decided, therefore, that formal interviews of these personnel would be carried out by the central team. This gave a useful 'second opinion' about professional centres and aspects of their operations and was useful in ensuring that the central team from Bristol was kept in contact with the scheme.

The second issue is the geographical separation of the central team from either of the action areas and while this remained a subject of concern, there appeared to be advantages and disadvantages. Without the presence of local evaluators, a central team removed from any base within the local area of the action scheme would have great difficulty in maintaining close contact. The schemes were too large and complex to allow attendance at the variety of meetings and activities taking place, and this is likely to be the case for other large-scale action programmes. This possibility, that a central team will become divorced, needs to be borne in mind if similar teams are established. We felt that it could happen, but regular meetings of the evaluation team, a good travel budget allowing a reasonable number of central visits to the schemes, the constant supply of reports and frequent telephone contacts helped us to combat the problem. One advantage in this central plus local evaluator approach was the fact that 'outsiders' could be brought in to conduct the interviews of those with whom the local evaluators have close contacts, which often takes them outside a purely evaluative stance.

The third issue, closely related to the above, concerns the role of the evaluation team in supplying 'feedback' on the schemes. Both local evaluators were emphatic that they needed immediate data, capable of rapid processing for feedback to the scheme organizers and the LEA Advisory Committee on Induction, the main representative body for the many groups involved in the scheme. Both issued a series of short evaluation reports dealing with specific aspects of their local scheme, e.g. reports on block release courses for the probationers, on probationer response to professional centre provision, on teacher-tutor views of their role, etc. The desire to obtain formative evaluation data sometimes meant that both a local questionnaire and a central team questionnaire arrived in schools within a very short space of time. On such occasions, our practice was to send the local questionnaire first, with a covering letter informing schools of the impending arrival of the 'national' questionnaire and requesting their co-operation.

The central team had a brief to disseminate information about the schemes as part of their evaluation contract with the DES. However, in portraying the schemes to audiences who knew little about them, despite frequent reservations, the evaluators seemed to be viewed as advocates of the scheme itself or a particular part of it, e.g. most often of the 'teacher-tutor' role. This particular concept was, of course, of central interest to teacher audiences, but many appeared to have difficulty in visualizing the operation of the role within their own particular school situation. In simply answering questions about the operationalization of the role within the schemes, one appeared to be recommending this concept for adoption. In reviewing this problem, the team decided that the continual making of caveats and reservations did not help the speakers' delivery or reception by the audience. We therefore asked what we ourselves did believe about the schemes and came to a broad agreement about this. Subsequently I personally found that prefacing my talk with a straight comment about my own views, indicating those elements for which I would cite supporting evidence and those which were subjective feelings arising from my own interpretations of conversations, seemed to remove the problem, almost invariably. Audiences were still critical, even taking the personal viewpoint to task, but it seemed to enable them to sort out the speaker's position, sift the evidence presented more clearly, and, strangely enough, allowed the speaker to adopt the evaluator stance more easily thereafter.

Two further issues, both relating to our questionnaires but having general application for other such evaluation exercises, may be noted. The most obvious was the problem of low response rate to postal qeustionnaires, which was interwoven with the problem of defining the sample to receive questionnaires. We sought the views of teachers both closely and only marginally involved in these schemes, seeking to assess the 'general' view of the schemes among experienced teachers in the pilot areas. For our sample, therefore, we sent questionnaires to all·schools in the schemes as follows: one for each probationer, the head, the teacher-tutor and one for a 'colleague' 'interested in' or 'affected by' the schemes. In primary schools deputy heads also received a questionnaire, but in secondary schools we sent questionnaires to one head of department for each probationer in that school. This formula did not always fit the particular circumstances of each school and the headteachers returned forms to let us know how many questionnaires had been distributed, and not all heads distributed questionnaires to their staff. This situation may differ between European countries, but in the United Kingdom it is normal to approach the schools in this way, through the headteacher. It does raise the problem, however, that teachers who might well have wanted to respond may be denied the opportunity to do so. This is clearly a professional issue for heads and others to resolve.

The response rate for those most directly involved was 68 per cent and in social science research this is an acceptable level of return on postal questionnaires. But reluctance to filling in questionnaires was apparent both on the returns ('My time is better spent teaching') and on the rejection slips ('Dear Researcher (sic), I am sorry that I cannot help you with this. We have too much to do this week (and every week.)')

So in these two LEAs, which had been given large government grants for action programmes intended to benefit new entrants to the profession, almost one-third of those most closely involved with the schemes did not assist the central evaluation team's first approach by questionnaire, and for the follow-up questionnaire, six months later, which was only two sides in length, the response rate dropped to 60 percent.

Among those who were only marginally connected with the schemes, there was a considerably lower response and the team decided not to approach this group (the 'colleague' category already noted) in the follow-up questionnaire. Many of the respondents wrote that they did not know much about the scheme and did not feel able to answer or comment upon it. This may tell us something about a lack of dissemination of information about the scheme which would be a pertinent comment on the management strategy for this innovation. On the other hand, that conclusion is only tendentious, for the explanation could just as easily be teacher reluctance to complete questionnaires in general, and it is to this latter problem that I wish to refer.

If, as I suspect, there are strong attitudinal prejudices among teachers against research generally, and against filling in questionnaires in particular, then there is no immediate panacea which will ensure even 95 percent response rates. The fact is that in most cases the teachers are in a poor position in relation to research and evaluation projects. They are asked to carry out the hard work in the action programme, and are cast in the role of guinea pigs to be studied by others. They are rarely involved in the evaluation side of projects except as respondents to time-consuming questionnaires. Since they seldom receive extra allowances of time for their involvement with research, there is frequent intrusion upon their private time. Worse still, the demand for their involvement in research and evaluation activities has increased, partly through the greater number of students now completing research theses (PhD, MEd, Advanced Diploma, etc.) and partly through the teachers' own demands for more directly relevant school or classroom-related research.

Despite the difficulties, however, teachers must be the principal source of information on many projects and, therefore, obtaining their views remains an integral part of the educational researcher's activities. To continue the present haphazard conduct of research approaches to schools within a prevailing climate not particularly sympathetic to research seems inadvisable and it is suggested that certain changes can be made which may be of benefit to the various parties involved. For European countries,

111

with similar problems, it is proposed that a local liaison structure and procedure is needed, e.g. through the formation of a representative committee within the LEA to monitor research approaches to the LEA's schools. Given the present move to school-focused research and the demands for public accountability of education, the professional associations and local authorities may find some such procedural arrangement not only more necessary but also valuable.

4.   EVALUATION IN YEAR 3

The third year of the evaluation programme consisted principally of in-depth case studies. The local evaluators studied particular schools and their induction programmes, particular tutors and their activities, etc. The central team conducted detailed case studies of various types of 'tutor' role, e.g. the 'external' tutor and the 'professional' tutor within schools having responsibility for all staff development rather than simply that of the probationers. To complete the evaluation, however, a review questionnaire was sent to all schools in the Northumberland and Liverpool LEAs, covering a wide sample of teachers involved in the schemes. Other questionnaires were sent to all the LEA advisers in both LEAs and a wide sample of the professional centre personnel. In this way, the team completed its policy of exploring the opinions of all parties actively involved in the schemes.

By the end of the third year of the scheme, school personnel may well have been suffering a degree of 'questionnaire-fatigue', and response rates did tend to decline. The evaluation team had taken this into account earlier and both local evaluators cut down their own approaches and tried to avoid overlap with the central team questionnaires. The central team limited itself to three questionnaires: none in year one, two in year two, and one at the end of year three. However, the actual number of questionnaires circulated was increased by the decision of the LEA organizers that they required their own surveys in addition to those supplied by the evaluation team. Further, the professional centres themselves began to use end-of-day (or course) questionnaires to obtain direct feedback about their courses. The latter development was interesting and the sheer volume of courses would have been too much for the local evaluators to take on. The evaluation team was not in a position to prevent this proliferation of questionnaires, and both the LEA and professional centre personnel had legitimate, cogent reasons for moving in this direction. It caused little immediate problem, but, as expected, the delayed cumulative result was increased dissatisfaction with filling in questionnaires.

The case studies from year three have to be set in the context of the evaluation programme as a whole, serving to enrich our knowledge by graphic examples of much that was brought to light by the questionnaire surveys. They raised some quite common problems such as the accumulation of an embarrassing mountain of data, some of which is of dubious value, and the sheer volume of which presents problems of analysis which may be underestimated by non-researchers. Also, we gave all institutions and indiviuduals a guarantee of anonymity, but to do so imposes constraints upon researchers in the presentation of data. Similar problems arise, too, from the nature of the data which, particularly in detailed case studies, may be highly personal and explosive. Other problems arise from working closely with teachers in the field. For example, it is frequently the case that the researcher is asked to comment on another interviewee by someone (e.g. another teacher) with whom the researcher is currently working and with whom he must continue to work. The questioner may be testing the researcher, or simply be asking in innocence without realizing the import of the question, or he may have Machiavellian motives. Unless an ethical view is immediately presented, the researcher's credibility as a confidante is destroyed and he could face difficult consequences depending upon the position taken by the questioner. Like the teacher, the researcher also has professional ethics and responsibility and these must be exercised carefully and for the benefit of the clients rather than the researcher's own interest.

Conclusions

Large-scale action research projects seldom have the time or opportunity to do all they would like to do in relation to the action programmes. The pressures of time, of shifts within the action programme, of calls for interim reports, of requests for dissemination, etc. all intrude upon the business of simply collecting and analysing data.

Data collection itself is not the simple process it is often conceived to be, by those not involved, and the problem of low response rates to postal questionnaires is a particularly significant one for social science researchers on large-scale projects. It was suggested earlier in the article that a regular structural and procedural system, e.g. a local liaison committee, might be beneficial and I wish to add a few explanatory comments.

Within our own project, the highest response rates came from the two LEAs who already had such a procedure. In the main schemes, a negotiation process with an ad hoc committee did take place, but there was no contact between this committee and the schools. Having a regular representative committee with this as one of its functions may be the way forward, but its existence and functions need to be made clear within the local school system.

The committee would consist minimally of representatives from the professional associations, the LEA and some providing agencies. It would probably be multifunctional and one of its functions (possibly delegated to a subcommittee) would be to ensure that schools were not overburdened with research approaches and that the instruments used were professionally acceptable to teachers. Minor modifications to wording or warnings of ambiguity might be suggested to the research representative, who would be present at the discussion of the instrument, but the technicalities of questions would, in the main, be left to the researchers. While researchers might view the existence of such a committee as a constraint, our experience suggests that this is only a limited constraint and that more is to be gained by open co-operation with the interested parties than by maintaining a research aloofness. If teachers are sure that their LEA and professional associations know about and have accepted the implications of research projects through such a regularized procedure, this may serve to defuse reactions against both specific research instruments and the research community generally.

In discussing some of the problems relating to the research activities undertaken by the TIPS Project team, I would not wish to suggest that our work has been bedevilled by problems. Far from it. We have been most fortunate in having active co-operation among a five-person evaluation team, with the action programme organizers, with the INIST[5] steering committee for the Project and have had an enthusiastic and astonishing degree of open co-operation from those involved with our case study work. I write this article, therefore, from the absolute conviction, brought about by the experience of the TIPS Project, that open co-operation between researcher, professional associations, LEA representatives and serving teachers will benefit not only the research enterprise, but also mutual understanding within the education system.

1.   For Northumberland: Mr C. McCabe, University of Newcastle upon Tyne; For Liverpool: Dr D. Hill, and then Dr J. Davis, University of Liverpool.

2.   Hereafter referred to as 'the central team' and comprising Dr R. Bolam. Mr K. Baker and later Miss A. McMahon.

3.   Details of these schemes may be found in: (a) DES Report on Education No. 84, (Great Britain, DES, 1976). (b) Baker, K. (1976.)

4.   Further detail on the conceptual framework and its application to the evaluation may be found in: (a) Bolam 1975(a). (b) Bolam, 1975(b).

5.   INIST - Induction and In-service Training Committee: a subcommittee of the National Advisory Committee on the Supply and Training of Teachers (ACSTT).

NATIONAL LEVEL
Central team at the University of Bristol

LOCAL LEVEL
Local Evaluators at the Universities of Liverpool and Newcastle-upon-Tyne

	NATIONAL LEVEL	LOCAL LEVEL
YEAR 1 1974-5 a)	(i) Field surveys of LEA induction approaches (ii) Pilot case studies of induction in schools in Liverpool, Northumberland and other LEAs (iii) Working conference-organizers and administrators from Liverpool, Northumberland and ten LEAs (iv) Production of National Conference Report 1975	(i) Field studies in schools-observation, interviews, diaries (ii) Attendance and observation at various committee meetings (iii) Questionnaire surveys to tutors, heads, probationers, etc. (iv) Attitude tests (Northumberland only) (v) Production of evaluation reports
YEAR 2 1975-6 b)	(i) Two national questionnaire surveys of school participants (Liverpool and Northumberland plus samples in 8 LEAs) (ii) Semi-structured interviews with professional centre and LEA Advisory Service personnel (iii) National Report - DES Report No. 84 (Great Britain, 1976)	Continuance of the above items Involvement in national questionnaire surveys, its data processing and National Report
YEAR 3 1976-7 c)	(i) Case studies of 'helping' roles in 3 LEAs: (a) 'staff tutors' within schools - Leeds; (b) visiting LEA 'advisory teachers' - Cumbria; (c) visiting 'external tutors' - ILEA, Division 8; Avon (ii) End of scheme questionnaires - school, professional centre and advisory personnel (iii) Opinion surveys through LEA Advisory Comms. seeking final views of the representatives of all the major groups involved (iv) National Report - DES Report No. 89 (Great Britain, 1977b) (v) Evaluation conference - September 1977	(i) Continuance of items in (a) above (ii) Involvement in national evaluation activities, e.g. end of project questionnaire (iii) Attitude surveys in both LEAs (iv) Case studies of particular tutors, probationers and schools (v) Local dissemination via a monthly Induction Newsletter (Liverpool only)
1977-8	Development of final reports Collating of extension year material	Monitoring of one year's extension of scheme with emphasis on tutors. Some 'retrospective' evaluation
1978-9	Collection of resource material and establishing of centre for dissemination (Conference June 1979) Final report prepared for DES (a further 3-year project)	Final reports published

Chapter Eight

EXTENSION OF THE THEME AND DISCUSSION OF SOME ISSUES

(a) Extension

The picture which results from the surveys and case studies is one which, I believe, shows the firmly based and promising condition of in-service evaluation in the United Kingdom. We see that techniques and examples are now available for evaluating in-service provision at a distance or in small, immediate groups, over long periods or short, involving teachers' centres or individual schools and for parts of programmes or co-ordinated national schemes, although it is well that Keith Baker reminds us in the last chapter that in this developing field examples like his are not claimed as 'models'.

The key word is perhaps 'promising'. There are excellent examples about but not as yet so many in the ordinary field of the bread-and-butter provision of practical courses for teachers.

The techniques and some teachers with the necessary skills are available, but are the schools and the in-service providers ready for them? If there were one theme I should want to pick out from the later case studies it would be this. Quite apart from the natural reluctance to complete question-naires and have new tasks added to their loads, teachers, whether presenting or attending courses, often see evaluation as both threat and burden. It is to some extent encouraging that this should be so, that we should have reached this stage. Once resistance to evaluation is met it means that it has reached the second order and gone beyond the anonymous, completely non-threatening 'please answer a few questions on your course' stage; it is becoming worthwhile and a full part of the process of in-service education. And this is what it must become if it is to be effective.

In the studies, John Davis refers particularly to such problems and diffi-culties and Roland Hoste is aware of them, but it is Chris Saville whose work faces them most firmly. If evaluation is to be of any use - and this is the great challenge facing both schools and in-service providers - then school organizations and teachers will have to open themselves to it and be educated not just to accept it and tolerate it, but to make it fully part of the process they are carrying on. This is the task Davis and Saville and Elliott, for example have started to tackle - in-service work with evalua-tion as both aim and process - and this is, I feel, now a most important development and need in in-service education in the United Kingdom.

I find myself impressed by what has been done in Suffolk. It is itself, of course, influenced by Elliott's work at Cambridge and the Ford Teaching Project, but for the most sophisticated example of its kind in the United Kingdom I believe it is necessary to look outside 'school' teacher in-service work to the medical field. To extend the main theme and because it could become something of a model for school-based development I turn to an in-service scheme to prepare the trainers of family doctors. Perhaps the closest parallel in school education terms would be courses to prepare teacher or professional tutors for work with new teachers in school.

Professor Furneaux, of Brunel University, outlined the scheme and its evaluation in this way:

> Our activities are mainly concerned with post-experience work with doctors. In this area of work, the most important enterprise has been in connection with our contract with the Royal College of General Practitioners, to collaborate in the design and evaluation of a series of experimental courses, organised and financed under the auspices of the Nuffield Provincial Hospitals Trust, which are intended to turn practising general practitioners into a relatively new kind of professional called a General Practitioner Trainer. This work is still in progress, and under the terms of our contract, no extended report can be made available until after the project has been completed, in about September of this year. Essentially, each course consists of a set of six full-time one-week residential modules, spaced at reasonably equal intervals throughout a year. The 20 or so GPs who attend each course work through the six modules in sequence, and emerge at the other end as people qualified to design, organise, contribute to, and monitor, various kinds of vocational training courses, for yet other GPs. The evaluation work is carried out by a member of our research staff, seconded to the Royal College for this purpose. Evaluation itself proceeds both in the illuminative and in the formal modes, and the general approach is that of a sort of modified action research. That is to say, the evaluator aims to provide insights for the course designer, while the modules are in progress, and also has an important supportive role with the 'students'.

> Nevertheless, at the same time, a variety of objective evaluation instruments are in use, providing data which will not fully be taken into account until after the end of the total programme.

The report which will probably be available in 1980 should be of great interest to the teaching profession in general.

An important part of the programme was that a good deal of work was expected from the participants between each module, but the group work was its key feature. By the time three of the block release courses had been held, over one hundred potential doctor-teachers had completed them and the pattern established was as follows.*

*I am grateful to Dr Freeling, Mrs Kaneti-Barry and Dr Irvine for discussing their work with me.

Each doctor-student found himself one of a small subgroup which provided a 'safe house' and support but demanded a change in attitude from confidence to questioning, honesty in assessment and ranking of self and others. The composition of the group would also be adjusted if it began to become too 'cosy'. These successful adults coming on the course with set roles and attitudes needed to be shaken in their roles, increase their flexibility, appreciate the emotional effects of the curriculum and so find their own strengths and weaknesses and how to use both. Process was at least as important as content and the work of the evaluator was integral to the group process. Mrs Susie Kaneti-Barry insisted that her role as non-medical participant observer, complementing that of Dr Paul Freeling as course organizer and presenter, could only be possible if she were involved in all courses right from their start.

Both set up firm constraints within which they must work. For example:

Nothing was included or done which was not a learning experience (and this included both assessment and evaluation).

Anything the organizer (or evaluator) did should be under the same constraints as was the work the group members are being prepared for. (e.g. if their learners would not be able to select their course members, then they should not select theirs).

Evaluation of teacher and course and all participants continued all the time. Emotional responses and the stages at which they were noted, the nature of judgements being made and the individual achievements of the groups were found to form identifiable patterns. The monitoring, recognition and bringing on of reactions was part of the process; the drop-out rate of this disturbingly intense group process was extremely low, and it appeared to be producing a highly active core of doctors spread all over the country fully ready to 'take the fire of teaching' (Freeling's phrase).

The evaluator, in looking at both organizers and course, provided feedback if crises were appearing or if what was developing appeared to run counter to the aims of the course so the evaluation was formative. The diagnostic evaluation was kept separate and given later. Again, of course, a major aim of the process was to involve everyone throughout and to enable them to carry out their own evaluations. Even in this the course was received developmentally and one's own resistance to evaluation was one of the processes to be learned and worked through...so the process was reflected throughout the process and the content came with it. Finally, as to testing, medical competency (content) tests were found to work in the opposite way to what might be expected, but in a long testing session, the Myer-Briggs Personality Inventory, the Eysenck Personality Inventory, an Intelligence Test (AH5) and Tough/Tendermindedness scales were given. Paired comparison tests for educational methods, and later, semantic differential and grid approaches to Maslow's and Tavistock classifications were also introduced. Course members as a result of this experience frequently produced and validated their own measures.

Clearly the funding and arrangements for this training scheme are different from those operated by either the local education authorities or the Department of Education and Science, but could this be the best mechanism for opening up a system to new ideas and evaluation? The future of in-service work for teachers may well lie in school-based programmes, indeed it is being more and more recognized that to be effective all in-service work must be in a sense school-based. The studies in this paper indicate that evaluation needs to be an integral part of both process and content of in-service courses. Is the way into this new development likely to be through the integrating role of a professional tutor in the school and a training course like this?

Elliott brings out an interesting range of methodological issues very clearly. He shows how personal they may be and how they affect and change the nature of an evaluation as it develops. But it is also clear that his solutions and problems arise from the nature of his task, his own principles and assumptions and the conditions under which he works, as well as that the stance he adopts could lead to conflict with, say, the body commissioning or approving the research. Baker's report on the other hand shows how careful an evaluator has to be not to identify himself too closely with any sectional interest in a large scale project, how difficult 'hard' data is to come by and how widely and fairly a net has to be cast to sample 'informed professional opinion' where the climate of opinion in schools and the views of non-involved teachers may be as important as those of participants. For these reasons the appointment of an involved but semi-detached team of evaluators seems necessary for the evaluation of large-scale innovation. Between these two extremes comes the whole range of approaches, from the simple, carefully designed questionnaire, given to a statistically valid sample and backed probably by structured interviews with critical items (Henderson, for example), to the most tentative steps illustrated in Davis's study, depending on the nature of the activity and its context - as well as who is seen as the consumer of the evaluation.

Whether case studies, historical, theoretical or portrayal in nature, are the best media for evaluation and its reporting, whether they should concentrate on individuals or organizations and what forms of participation should be encouraged are wider questions addressed by Fox (1979) in his (forthcoming) monograph 'Reflecting upon INSET evaluation'. They are issues for further discussion. So too are the roles of the evaluator as interpreter and something like psychotherapist.

The treatment of practical issues must here be limited to two constraints upon in-service evaluation. The first of these is time in which to do the work, when time is the most expensive commodity in in-service provision. The North Suffolk case study shows how much preparation, teaching time and follow-up goes into a simple evaluation course; the time-consuming nature of Elliott's commitment is clear and the vast amount of evaluators' and secretarial work which is involved in the Induction Pilot Project evaluation procedures must be stressed. All these studies describe work which involved commissioned professional evaluators, and were yet pressed for time, both to collect and process data and even more to produce reports when needed, for in practical terms evaluation only becomes effective when a report is in the right hands at the right time. It cannot be emphasized enough that evaluation is not a spare-time activity, or an extra. The theories, techniques and methodologies behind it have to be considered seriously and time has to be allocated for it. The all-too-common result of its not being taken seriously in time-allocations is that it stays at the first order, if indeed the questionnaire returns are processed at all. Should this time be given to course organizers or should special evaluators be brought in? It depends upon the context...there should be no difference from the point of view of expense...Davis's and Elliott's developments for example should become self-monitoring, some of the institutions mentioned by Taylor find having a service appropriate, wider national projects probably need a team carrying out evaluation as a research project with a definite time-scale.

Secondly, finance. The provision of time is, as we have seen, the main expense of evaluation, but implicit in many of the case studies is the need to have secretarial assistance, and money for paper, postage and travel, as well as for arranging conferences which are often the best way to publicize findings. It has become commonplace to say that the four equal ingredients of a teaching activity are aims, context, method and evaluation, and that the last never gets its fair share of time or resources, but this need not be too expensive to rectify - the cost of the evaluation of one section of the teacher induction project was less than 5 percent of the total budget, for example.

The first part of this final section dealt with the need to create the right climate for evaluation in our schools, and with the possibility of having more in-service courses and activities designed to encourage the study of evaluation, more explicit self-monitoring and perhaps more sense of accountability among teachers. The second part indicates that for the evaluation of in-service activity to be effective, adequate resources must be put into it so that it is seen as an integral part of the provision. But more than that, evaluation requires individuals with a knowledge of techniques who have considered the theoretical bases of their work, can appreciate and construct methodologies and carry them out to a deadline. And for these we look once more to in-service courses, especially, this time, the promising developments in higher degree work in this important field. So the end is the beginning.

BIBLIOGRAPHY

ADELMAN, C. and ELLIOTT, J. (1975). 'Reflecting where the action is: The design of the Ford Teaching Project', *Education for Teaching*, 92, 8-20.

ADELMAN, C. and ELLIOTT, J. (1976). *Innovation at the Classroom Level. Unit 28.* (Bletchely: Open University Press. (E203)

APPLEBEE, A., HEAP, B., PERROTT, E. and WATSON, F. (1975). 'Changes in Teaching behaviour after completing a self-instructional micro-teaching Course'. *Journal of Programmed Learning and Educational Technology*, 12, 6, 348-61.

ARNOLD, R., GRAYSTONE, J.A., HUGHES, G. and POWELL, R. (1977). 'Wheels within wheels', *Times Educ. Suppl.* 4 November.

ASBURY, G. (1975). 'Evaluation of a one-term Reading and Language Arts Course', *British Journal of In-service Education*, 1, 3, 50-3.

AUGSTEIN, S., and THOMAS, L. (1973). *Educational Studies: a Post Experience Course. Reading Development. Unit 7. Developing your own Reading.* (Bletchley: Open University Press.)

BAKER, K. (1976). 'A Review of Current Induction Programmes for New Teachers', *British Journal of In-Service Education*, 2, 3.

BAKER, K. (1977). Project proposal: Evaluation of school-focused INSET. School of Education, University of Bristol.

BATES, A.W. (1974). 'The role of the tutor in evaluating distance teaching', *Teaching at a Distance*, 1, 35-40.

BLACKLOCK, S. (1976). 'Workload'. Open University, Survey Research Department. (mimeographed).

BOLAM, R. (1973). Induction programmes for teachers. Bristol School of Education, University of Bristol.

BOLAM, R. (1975a). 'The management of educational change towards a conceptual framework'. In: HOUGHTON, V.P., McHUGH, C.A.R., and MORGAN, C. (Eds) *Management in Education Reader 1: The Management of Organisations and Individuals.* London: Ward Lock. Also, in: HARRIS, A. LAWN, M, and PRESCOTT, W. (Eds) *Curriculum Design and development Reader 1: Curriculum Innovation* : Croom-Helm.

BOLAM, R. (1975b). 'The Teacher Induction Pilot Schemes Project', *London Educational Review*, 4, 1.

BOLAM, R. (1976). Innovative induction programmes: A study of factors affecting the design implementation, and evaluation of induction programmes for beginning teachers in four LEAs. Unpublished PhD thesis. University of Bristol.

BOLAM, R. (1976). *'Innovation in in-service education and training of teachers in the United Kingdom'.* Paris: OECD/Centre for Educational Research and Innovation.

BOLAM, R. (1978). *Innovation in the in-service education and training of teachers: Practice and theory*. Paris: OECD.

BOLAM, R., SMITH, G. and CANTER, H. (1976). The LEA Adviser and educational innovation. Bristol School of Education, University of Bristol.

BORICH, G.D. (1978). *The Evaluation of INSET for Teachers*. Paris: OECD.

BRADLEY, H.W. (1974). In-service education after the White Paper. School of Education, University of Nottingham.

BRADLEY, H. and EGGLESTON, J.F. (1977). An induction year experiment. School of Education, University of Nottingham.

BRADBURY, P.S. and RAMSDEN, P. (1975). Student evaluation of teaching at North East London Polytechnic. Paper presented to the University of London Institute of Education Conference on the Evaluation of Teaching in Higher Education. In: *Evaluating Teaching in Higher Education* University of London, Institute of Education.

BURGOYNE, J. and STUART, R. (1977). 'Implicit learning theories as determinants of the effect of management development programmes', *Personnel Review*, 6, 2, 5-14.

CAMBRIDGE INSTITUTE OF EDUCATION (1974). In-service courses and teacher opinion. The results of an inquiry into courses leading to the Certificate of Further Professional Study of the Cambrdige Institute.

CAMPBELL, D.T. and STANLEY, C.S. (1963). 'Experimental and quasi-experimental designs for research on teaching'. In: GAGE, N.L. (Ed) *Handbook of Research on Teaching*. Chicago: Rand McNally.

CANE, B. (1969). *In-service Training*. Slough: NFER.

CANTER, H. (1978) *Educational support agencies project report*. (Bristol School of Education, University of Bristol).

CHANAN, G. and DELAMONT, S. (1975). *Frontiers of classroom research*. Windsor: NFER Publishing Co.

COLLIER, G., MILLER, P. and WHITTAKER, R. (1977). 'One college's evaluation. Keswick Hall', *Evaluation Newsletter*, 4, 2-9.

COOPER, D. (1975). Reflecting where the action is. Unpublished paper relating to the evaluation of a conference in connection with the Ford Teaching Project.

COOPER, D. (1976). Conference Evaluation. Unpublished paper.

COOPER, J.M., WEBER, W.A. and JOHNSON, C.E. (Eds) (1973). *Competency based teacher education: 2. A systems approach to programme design*. McCutchan. Berkley, California.

COOPER, K. and SELLORS, W. (1977). 'Evaluation of an in-service course; The course tutor's views', *British Journal of In-service Education*, 4, 1/2, 90-2.

CRIX, B. (1976). 'Objectives and Evaluation of in-service education'. Courses viewed in the light of Blooms Taxonomy', *British Journal of In-service Education,* 2, 2, 106-12.

DAVEY, P. (1975). *PE261 - Reading Development; Course Feedback for 1974.* Bletchley: Open University, Survey Research Department. (mimeographed).

DAVIS, J. (1979). The Liverpool Induction Pilot Scheme: A summative report. University of Liverpool.

DELAMONT, S. (1976). *Interaction in the classroom.* London: Methuen.

DELAMONT, S. and STUBBS, M. (1976). *Explorations in the classroom.* London: Wiley.

DIDSBURY COLLEGE OF EDUCATION (1976). Course evaluation and Didsbury College

DOE, B. (1976). 'COSTA cuts across the curriculum to save ailing subject associations', *Times Educational Suppl.* 12 March.

ELLIOTT, J. (1977) (with a reply from Wynne Harlen). *Interim Working paper vi. From Project to LEAs.* Part 1 'Negotiating Dissemination Patterns with LEAs'. London: Schools Council Progress in Learning Science Project. (mimeographed).

ELLIOTT, J. (1977). *Interim Working Paper viii. Thinking Aloud: about the transactions between a curriculum development project and its sponsor.* London: Schools Council Progress in Learning Science Project. (mimeographed).

ELLIOTT, J. (1977a). 'Conceptualising relationships between research/ evaluation procedures and in-service teacher education', *British Journal of In-service Education,* 4, 1/2, 102-15.

ELLIOTT, J. (1977b). Evaluating in-service activities: From above or below? Cambridge Institute of Education. (mimeographed).

ELLIOTT, J. (1976). Evaluating the progress in learning Science dissemination. Unpublished paper.

ELLIOTT, J. et al. (1974). Ford teaching project units. University of East Anglia.

ELLIOTT, J. and ADELMAN, C. (1973). 'Reflecting where the action is: the design of the Ford Teaching Project', *Education for Teaching,* 92, 8-20.

ELLIOTT, J. and BRIDGES, D. (1977). *Interime Working Paper vii. From Project to LEAs.* Part 2. London: Schools Council Progress in Learning Science Project. (mimeographed).

ELLIS, J. (1975). Report on PE261: Follow-up. Open University. (mimeographed).

EVALUATION NEWSLETTER. Nos. 1, 2, 3, 4. Guildford: Society for Research into Higher Education and Committee for Research into Teacher Education.

FARNES, N.C. (1974). Interim report on an end of course questionnaire for PE261 (Reading Development). Open University. (mimeographed).

FILSTEAD, W.J. (1970). *Qualitative Methodology*. Chicago: Rand McNally.

FLANDERS, N.A. (1962). 'Using Interaction analysis in the in-service training of teachers', *Journal of Experimental Education*, 30, 313-6.

FOX, G.T. (Ed) (1976). Evaluating teacher education. 1975 CMTI Impact Study. Papers for American Educational Research Association (AERA) conference, Madison, University of Wisconsin-Madison.

FOX, G.T. (1977). Limitations of a standard perspective on programme evaluation: The example of ten years of teacher corps evaluation. Madison, University of Wisconsin-Madison.

FOX, G.T. and HERNANDEZ-NIETO, R. (1977). Why not quantitative methodologies to illuminate dialectical or phenomenological perspectives? Draft paper for Americal Educational Research Association (AERA) conference. Madison, University of Wisconsin-Madison.

FOX, G.T. (1979). *Reflecting upon INSET Evaluation*. Paris: OECD.

FULLAN, M. and POMFRET, A. (1977). 'Research on curriculum and instruction implementation', *Review of Educational Research*, 47, 2, 335-97.

GARNHAM et al. (1975). *The in-service needs of Gloucestershire teachers*. (Gloucestershire Co. Council).

GIBSON, D.R. (1974). Evaluation report of an in-service course for professional tutors. Cambridge Institute of Education.

GRAY, W. (1973). In-service training - Expectations and Achievements. Unpublished MEd, University of Birmingham.

GREAT BRITAIN. *Department of Education and Science (1972)*. *Education: A Framework for Expansion* London HMSO (Cmmnd. 5174).

GREAT BRITAIN. *Department of Education and Science (1976)*. 'Helping new Teachers: the Induction Year', *DES Report on Education*, No. 84.

GREAT BRITAIN. *Department of Education and Science (1977a)*. 'In-service training: the role of colleges and departments', *DES Report on Education*, No. 88.

GREAT BRITAIN. *Department of Education and Science (1978)* Making INSET work. London: HMSO.

GREAT BRITAIN. *Department of Education and Science (1977b)*. 'Teacher Induction: Pilot Schemes Progress', *DES Report on Education*, No. 89.

GREAT BRITAIN. *Parliament House of Commons (1977c)*. *Education in Schools: a Consultative Document*. London: HMSO (Cmmnd. 6869).

GREAT BRITAIN. *Scottish Education Department National Committee for the In-Service Training of Teachers (1975). Survey of In-service Training.* Edinburgh: Scottish Education Department.

GREENFIELD, T.B. (1975). 'Theory about organisation: a new perspective and its implications for schools'. In: M. HUGHES (Ed) *Administering Education: An International Challenge.* London: Athlone Press.

GUILFORD, J.P. and FRUCHTER, B. (1956). *Fundamental Statistics in Psychology and Education.* New York: McGraw Hill.

HAMILTON, D. (1976). *Curriculum Evaluation.* London: Open Books.

HAMILTON, D., JENKINS, D., KING, C., MACDONALD, B. and PARLETT, M. (Eds) (1977). *Beyond the number game: A reader in educational evaluation.* London: Macmillan.

HAMMOND, G. (1975). A survey of ATO/DES courses 1971-74. University of Exeter, School of Education.

HEMPHILL, J.K. (1969). 'The relationship between research and evaluation studies'. In: *National Society for the Study of Education, Educational Evaluation, New Roles and Means.* Chicago: University of Chicago Press.

HENDERSON, E.S. (1975). Some personal and school outcomes of in-service training. Unpublished PhD, University of Reading.

HENDERSON, E.S. (1976a). 'Attitude change in in-service education', *British Journal of In-service Education,* 2, 2, 113-6.

HENDERSON, E.S. (1976b). 'An investigation of some outcomes of in-service training', *British Journal of In-service Education,* 3, 1, 4-17.

HENDERSON, E.S. (1978). *The evaluation of in-service teacher training.* London: Croom Helm.

HENDERSON, E.S., PERRY, G.W. and SPENCER, M. (1975). The Co-ordination of in-service training for teachers. Department of Educational Studies, University of Oxford.

HOSTE, R. (1975). 'Evaluation in the college context', *Education for Teaching,* 97, 19-24.

HOSTE, R. (1976). Evaluating the physical education course. Unpublished paper.

HOUSE, E. (1972). 'The conscience of educational evaluation'. *Teachers College Record,* 73, 3.

HOYLE, E. (1976). *Innovation and the school, Unit 29.* Bletchley: Open University Press. (E203).

HOYLE, E. (1976). 'The PGCE Course: possibilities for research', *British Journal of Teacher Education,* 2, 87-94.

HUDSON, L. (1972). *The cult of the fact*. London: Cape.

HUNTER, E., and MERRITT, J. (1973). *"Individual progress in reading."*
(PE261: Reading Development, Units 12-13). (Open University Press).

JAMES, C.N. (1975). The Ealing Pilot Induction Scheme. Unpublished report,
University of London Institute of Education.

JAMES REPORT. GREAT BRITAIN. *Department of Education and Science (1972).*
Teacher Education and Training. London: HMSO.

JENKINS, D. (1976). *Curriculum evaluation. Unit 20.* Bletchley: Open
University Press. (E203).

JORDANHILL COLLEGE OF EDUCATION (1977). Four term in-service courses for
the award of a Post-graduate Diploma in Educational Technology.
College submission to the Council for National Academic Awards.

KEAST, D.J. and CARR, V. (1979). 'School based INSET: Interim Evaluation',
British Journal of In-service Education, 5, 3, 25-31.

LAWN, M. (1974). Enquiry into Resources and Reading. Open University
Press (mimeographed).

LYNCH, J. (1977). Lifelong education and the preparation of educational
personnel. UNESCO Institute of Education, Hamburg.

MacDONALD, B. (1976a). 'Evaluation and the control of education'. In:
D. TAWNEY (Ed) *Curriculum Evaluation Today: Trends and Implications.*
London: Macmillan.

MacDONALD, B., and WALKER, R. (1976b). *The portrayal of persons as*
evaluation data. An American Educational Research Association (AERA)
paper, University of East Anglia, (Norwich), Centre for Applied
Research in Education.

MacDONALD, B., and WALKER, R. (1976). *Changing the curriculum.* London:
Open Books.

MacDONALD, B. et al. (1974). Innovation, evaluation, research and the
problem of control. SAFARI Project, University of East Anglia.

McCABE, C. (1977). 'Attitude scales and continuing evaluation', *Evaluation*
Newsletter, 4, 16-9.

McCABE, C. (1978). Induction in Northumberland: An Evaluation. University
of Newcastle, School of Education.

McCABE, C. (1978). *The Evaluation of INSET in the United Kingdom.* Paris:
OECD (incorporated in present text).

McCORMICK, B. (1976). Course evaluation and course production. Unpublished paper.

McHUGH, G.A.R. (1974). Course PE261 - Reading Development: End of course survey of student implementation of ideas and techniques discussed in the course. Open University. (mimeographed).

McINTOSH, N. (1974). 'Some problems involved in the evaluation of multi-media educational systems', *British Journal of Educational Technology*, 3, 5, 43-59.

McINTYRE, D., and MacLEOD, G. (1977). *The characteristics and uses of systematic classroom observation*. University of Stirling, for British Educational Research Association Conference (mimeographed).

McNAMARA, D. (1973). 'An approach to evaluating an innovatory course in colleges of education', *Durham Research Review*, 30, 762-7.

McNAMARA, D. (1975. 'Curriculum evaluation: A critical overview'. *Educational Studies*, 1, 2. 93-8.

McNAMARA, D. (1975). *Final report of the applied education project*. University of Lancaster, School of Education.

MAXWELL, A.E. (1970). *Basic statistics in behavioural research*. London: Penguin.

MOORE, J. (1974). CT4 Tutor feedback scheme 1974: Course PE261. Four reports, Open University (mimeographed).

MOSER, C.A., and KALTON, G. (1971). *Survey methods in social investigation*. London: Heinemann.

MOYLE, D. (1973). *The reading curriculum (PE261: Reading Development, Units 10-11)*. Bletchley: Open University Press.

OPEN UNIVERSITY (1972). *Post-experience course prospectus*. Bletchley: Open University Press.

OPEN UNIVERSITY (1976). *Course Handbook 1976*. Bletchley: Open University Press.

PARLETT, M., and HAMILTON, D. (1976). 'Evaluation as illumination: a new approach to the study of innovatory programmes'. In TAWNEY, D. (Ed) *Curriculum Evaluation Today: Trends and Implications*. London: MacMillan.

PERROTT, E. (1977). *Self-instructional micro-teaching courses for in-service teachers*. Micro-teaching Research Unit, University of Lancaster, for Committee for Research in Teacher Education (CRITE) seminar (mimeographed).

RILEY, J. (1976). 'Course teams at the Open University'. *Studies in Higher Education* 1, 1, 57-61. Also in: SQUIRES, G. (Ed) *Course teams: Four case Studies and a commentary*. London: Nuffield Foundation.

RUTHERFORD, W.L. and WEAVER, S.W. (1974). 'Preferences of elementary teachers for preservice and in-service training in the teaching of reading', *Educ. Res.*, 67, 6, 271-5.

SCHOOLS COUNCIL (1980). *Progress in Learning Science. Final Report* (Part III). 'Portrait of a Project'. (mimeographed).

SCHOOLS COUNCIL RESEARCH STUDIES (1973). *Evaluation in Curriculum Development: 12 Case Studies*. London: Macmillan.

SCHWARTZ, H., CICHON, D., JAMES, K., MELNICK, C. and OLSON, G. (1977). The use of multiple research methodologies to evaluate an in-service curriculum. American Educational Research Association (AERA) conference paper (College of Education, Roosevelt University, Chicago).

SCRIVEN, M. (1967). 'The methodology of evaluation'. In: TYLER, R.W., GAGNE, R.M. and SCRIVEN, M. *Perspectives on curriculum evaluation*. American Educational Research Association (AERA), Monograph on Curriculum Evaluation No. 1. Chicago: Rand McNally.

SHIPMAN, M. (1979). *In-school Evaluation*. London: Heinemann.

SIEGEL, S. (1956). *Nonparametric statistics for the behavioural sciences*. New York: McGraw Hill.

SMITH, J. (1975). 'An evaluation of an in-service course. Case studies in the primary school'. *British Journal of In-service Education*, 1, 2.

SMITH, R.A. (Ed) (1975). *Regaining educational leadership: Critical essays on PBTE/CBTE Behavioural objectives and accountability*. London:Wiley.

SMITH, R.J. et al. (1970). 'Elementary teachers' preferences for pre-service and in-service training in the teaching of reading'. *Educ. Res.*, 63, 445-9.

STAKE, R. (1976). *Evaluating educational programmes: The need and the response*. Paris: OECD.

STEADMAN, S. (1976). 'Techniques of evaluation'. In: TAWNEY, D. (Ed) *Curriculum Evaluation Today: Trends and Implications*. London: Macmillan.

STOCKHAUSEN, K.G. (1973). Forward in: De la GRANGE, *Mahler*. London: Gollantz.

STONES, E. (1973). 'Comments on Professor Taylor's lecture', *Council of Europe Information Bulletin*, 3, 42-4. Symposium on Research and Reform in Teacher Education. Strasbourg: Documentation Centre for Education in Europe.

STUFFLEBEAM, D. et al. (1971). *Educational evaluation and decision making*. Itasca, Illinois: F.E. Peacock.

TAWNEY, D. (Ed) (1976). *Curriculum evaluation today: Trends and Implications*. London: Macmillan.

TAYLOR, J.K. and DALE, I.R. (1971). A survey of teachers in their first year of service. University of Bristol, School of Education.

TAYLOR, L. (1973). Survey of primary school teachers opinions on in-service training. Mather College of Education, Manchester.

TAYLOR, P.W. (1977). In-service education and training of teachers. A review of evaluation practices in the United Kingdom. University of Bristol, School of Education.

TOWNSEND, H.E.R. (1970). 'The in-service training of teachers in primary and secondary schools'. In: GREAT BRITAIN. *Department of Education and Science. Statistics of Education, Special Series 2:* Survey of In-service Training for Teachers 1967. London: HMSO.

TURNER, R.L. (Ed) (1973). Performance education: A general catalogue of teaching skills. Syracuse University, School of Education.

WALTON, J. (Ed) (1974). *ATO/DES courses 1973/4: An Evaluation.* University of Exeter, School of Education, (mimeographed).

WILSON, J. (1979). *Fantasy and Common sense in Education.* Oxford: Martin Robertson.

ZELDITCH, M. (1962). 'Some methodology problems of field studies'. *American Journal of Sociology.* 67, 266-76.